Don't Stop Now

Making the Most of the Rest of Your Life

Jan Fishler, MA & L. Gianforte

Cover and book design by Patty Arnold, *Menagerie Design & Publishing*
menageriedesign.net

Author photos by Kim Sayre, kimsayrephotography.com

Published by Tin Cat Media, Nevada City, California

ISBN: 978-0-9826723-4-1

Some of the anecdotal illustrations in this book are true to life and are included with the permission of the persons involved. All other illustrations are composites of real situations, and any resemblance to people living or dead is coincidental.

Library of Congress Control Number: 2018908117

"Step out of the history that is holding you back. Step into the new story you are willing to create."

— Oprah Winfrey, American media proprietor

To every woman who chooses to rage against the dying of the light

"Do not go gentle into that good night,
Old age should burn and rave at close of day;
Rage, rage against the dying of the light." —Dylan Thomas

ACKNOWLEDGMENTS

An enormous thank you to the women who shared their stories for our features: Arleen Hiuga, Judi Townsend, Wendy Satsky, Janice O'Brien, and Cheryl Acheson. A celestial hug to Natalie Hoogasian, who lives on in our hearts.

A deep debt of gratitude to our experts: Dr. Anita Mukherjee; Dr. Kweethai Neill; and Dr. Matthew Muellenhoff, who has the distinction of being the only male in this book.

Elan Bongiorno, Kerry Herta, Jamie Haynes, Julie Morgan, and Amy Nadine Clement jumped in with priceless beauty tips, and for that we are forever grateful. (And now we know how to be knockouts at any age.)

A big shout-out to all of our female friends and acquaintances who didn't even know their stories were fodder for this book.

Patty Arnold dazzled us once again with her fabulous design skills, and she always seems to know precisely what we want even when we can't articulate it. Proofreader extraordinaire Kit Bailey is skilled at finding even the teeniest mistakes, so if you spot a typo, it's all his fault.

Table of Contents

Preface   ix

Introduction   Personal Assessment   xiii

Chapter 1   Being Kind to Your Body—Even If It's Not Being Kind to You   1

Chapter 2   Emotional Rescue   13

Chapter 3   Money Management 101   29

Chapter 4   Lovers and Children and Friends, Oh My!   39

Chapter 5   Ain't Misbehavin'—or Are You?   53

Chapter 6   Putting Your Best Face—and Other Body Parts—Forward   71

Chapter 7   Learning—It's Not Just for Kids   87

Chapter 8   Tapping into Generosity   97

Chapter 9   Putting It All Together   107

Addendum   Creating Your Plan   121

Endnotes   122

About the Authors   124

Preface

Look over your shoulder. Who do you see? A cool college coed? A successful businesswoman? A meticulous homemaker? A devoted wife? An adoring mother? A respected member of the community?

Now look in the mirror. Are any of those women still there, or is nothing left but their shadows?

Let's be honest here, ladies. We're in the second half of our lives, and it's probably the most confusing era we've ever experienced. We've accomplished a lot to date—much of it sweetly, satisfyingly mundane; some of it dramatically impressive—but where do we go from here?

For years, we've worked hard—in business, at home, as volunteers. We've been contributing members of society throughout our adult lives, and now the questions loom: *What's next? Is that all there is? Have I done enough? Do I have it in me to do more?*

By the age of fifty-five or so, we tumble gracelessly into the category of senior. What does that even mean? In its best iteration, it translates to a 10 percent discount at Ross every Tuesday; ordering off the senior menu at Denny's, which is nothing more than smaller portions; carrying an AARP membership card, demonstrating proof that we're officially old; and getting a free pass to Silver Sneakers if we have the appropriate supplemental insurance. Big whoop.

Our generation was raised on sex, drugs, and rock 'n' roll, and many of us who survived still have some of that wild energy to burn. Clearly, a mini stack of blueberry pancakes at 5:30 p.m. isn't going to cut it. We want to continue to be involved, excited, and enthusiastic about life in ways that have meaning to us and to our loved ones.

Some women find great satisfaction in helping to raise their grandchildren, but there are others who want that—and more. Remember what it felt like to go to your first rock concert, to see a light show, to backpack through Europe? That person is still buried in there somewhere, and she wants to get out really, really badly. She wants to capture life and enjoy all the time she has left. She wants to leave a mark, letting the world know she has made a difference—however small it might be.

Aging is not for sissies. We can't just sit back and hope that something wonderful will suddenly happen. Gone are the days when fresh, sparkling youth might have opened doors of opportunity. As years pass, we must work harder to find what fulfills us. We're exploring uncharted territory, to be sure, but it still harbors secrets, delights, and promises. It's simply up to us to find them.

As we move into this unknown future, we have choices to make. Will we accept the invisibility that plagues women as age diminishes beauty and disguises character? Will we stop pushing our bodies into fitness because it's starting to hurt too much? Will we give our brains a break from work? Will we simply let go and give up? Or will we continue to figure out ways to grow—bringing vital, creative contributions to our world and expanding the definition of age-appropriate?

There are no right or wrong answers to these questions, because the aging process is a different journey for each of us. Some of us have physical conditions that prevent our bodies from moving as we'd like. Others have financial constraints that keep dreams at bay. But life is more about attitude than accounting. It's about seizing what's at our disposal and making it work for us. It's about doing what we love as often as possible until we are forced to stop.

MAKING THE MOST OF THE REST OF YOUR LIFE

Attitude is one of the few things that is ours alone. When we take control of our attitude, we take control of our life.

As we age, we tend to lose control over many things. We slow down, our reflexes aren't what they used to be, and our bodies begin to fail us. We can't walk as far or stay up as late as we used to. We stop driving at night because our vision isn't very sharp. Memory loss sets in, and we lose names to familiar faces, forget book and movie titles, and repeat ourselves. We begin to complain, and eventually we might complain a lot because we don't feel as good as we want to. We chalk it all up to aging, and some of us are just plain bitter and pissed off at what is simply part of the living process.

So how do we rage against the inevitable? How can we be happy in this stage of our lives given the issues that can't be avoided?

We'll let you in on a little secret we learned from Martha Washington: "The greater part of our happiness or misery depends upon our dispositions, and not upon our circumstances." In other words, cultivate a positive attitude. Stop bitching and complaining and start being curious, enthusiastic, attentive and—how's this for a concept?—interesting! Most important of all, have fun—and not just once in a while. Do something enjoyable. Every. Single. Day.

Take a moment now to think about your idea of fun. Is it an early-morning walk before your neighborhood is awake? Running with your dog in the woods? Lingering in bed on Sundays watching Netflix? Enjoying fine dining? Shopping for shoes? Lunching with the girls? Organizing your closet? Spending hours working in the garden? Write down the things that make you happy.

Make a point of experiencing some of life's little pleasures each day. And perhaps once a month, do something special. Maybe it's a weekend of theatre and museums in the closest major city. A visit to a beach town. A trip to wine country. Antiquing. The symphony or a rock concert. Whatever sets your heart aflutter.

DISCOVERING STRATEGIES

To help you find your way through the maze of life after fifty, this book will provide tips, suggestions, and inspiration. We'll share the behaviors that have proved fruitful and steer you away from the ones that are head-bangingly ineffective. We'll introduce you to real women who've discovered real solutions to the dilemmas that plague us as we make our way through the rest of our lives. They share their stories with a frank openness, demonstrating a sweet sisterhood that links us all together.

Personal Assessment

Cynthia and Barbara were chatting over coffee at their neighborhood cafe. Cynthia was complaining bitterly about her life: thankless work, thoughtless husband, entitled kids, and excess weight. Barbara, sympathy written all over her face, sipped her latte and listened. Sadly, she'd heard it all before. The complaining never ceased; the story hardly changed. Here they were again—two old friends, from similar backgrounds. Yet one sees the proverbial glass half empty, while the other sees it half full.

All of us are somewhere along this continuum—maybe Little Miss Sunshine, maybe Eeyore from *Winnie the Pooh*. The first step is to find out where. Once you know where you stand, you can decide what you're going to do about it—if anything.

To get you started, we present a series of assessment statements at the beginning of each chapter. Each statement addresses a specific area of life:

1. Physical Wellness

2. Emotional Health

3. Finances

4. Relationships

5. Behaviors

6. Appearance

7. Learning Something New

8. Giving Back

We're going to ask you to think about each one, and then rate it on a scale of 1 to 10. A rating of 1 means "Alas, this isn't even remotely true" and 10 means "OMG! It's like you know me!" The numbers you choose are indicators of your emotional and physical state, and they may vary a bit from day to day. For now, choose the number that best reflects your feelings when you take the assessment. You might be pleasantly surprised at how much you've accomplished and how good you feel about your life.

Keep in mind that sometimes all it takes to feel better and be better is an adjustment in perception. Other times, a more proactive change is required. The goal of this assessment is to identify areas where you can make improvements, define the steps required to do so, and appreciate how far you've come.

BEING OPEN TO CHANGE

The good news: if there is one thing we can count on in life, it's change. Kids grow up and eventually leave the house. The boss you hate working for finally retires. Your best friend moves to Iowa, and while you're mourning the loss, you make new friends at a knitting group. You finally quit smoking. Your extremely frugal spouse dies, and in the file with his life insurance policy, you find $20,000 in small bills with a note telling you to take a great vacation. We never know what's around the next corner, so why not be open to the possibilities?

In too many cases, we inadvertently close ourselves off and miss out on what the future might present. We're afraid to look forward and afraid to look back, so we fail to see our strides and our successes. We're so busy with the tasks at hand that we forget to acknowledge the little things that make life wonderful. We complain and fail to be grateful for what we have.

By completing the assessments with an honesty that is usually reserved for a wine-fueled evening with your best friend, you just might emerge with a clearer picture of your life, where it seems to be headed, and whether you want to shift course.

If all your assessments on a specific topic are in the 9 to 10 range, clearly you are a rock star in that arena of your life. If you fall at the lower or middle end of the spectrum, there's work that can be done to make your situation better. It's completely up to you. We'll provide suggestions on things you can do to move up the scale and feel better about your life. We'll also share stories of women who've been where you are, pushed through their self-erected walls, and emerged happier and more fulfilled.

At the end of each chapter, you'll find recommendations for actions you can take to improve your circumstances. Think of it as the accountability portion of this book. We'll ask you to commit to specific steps that will get you going in the right direction, and we encourage you to add more steps of your own. While we'd love to be there to help keep you on track, this part is solely up to you.

If it's tough for you to get going on your own, consider joining a support group. Whether the unifying factor is coping with physical health or breaking bad habits, a support group is the place to find others who are facing the same challenges. The camaraderie of women is incredibly powerful, and you're likely to find the understanding and inspiration you need to get a better grasp on your circumstances and/or light a fire under your butt.

Rebecca was diagnosed with breast cancer at the age of sixty-eight. For six months, she put her head down and plunged through the process: selecting doctors, firing doctors, doing the necessary research, submitting to the invasive tests, and finally undergoing a bilateral mastectomy. Her husband was by her side every step of the way, and she took comfort in that—so much so that she never took the time to truly assess her feelings. When her oncologist sympathetically asked her how it felt to lose an erogenous zone, she was momentarily shocked by the question. She didn't realize until that moment that she had even lost one.

This was a wake-up call for her, and she started to think about the grieving she'd failed to do. She knew it was an essential part of her healing, so she joined a cancer support group for women.

"Everything changed after that," she told us. "Every single fear, concern, or crazy thought I'd had since my diagnosis was shared by at least one other person in the group. It was so clear to me that I was exactly where I needed to be."

So don't feel as if you have to do the work alone. Seek help from a family member, good friend, or a room full of fabulous strangers. Whatever works. If you really want to make the most of the rest of your life, there's a variety of different ways to take action.

Chapter 1

Being Kind to Your Body— Even If It's Not Being Kind to You

"Communities and countries and ultimately the world are only as strong as the health of their women." —Michelle Obama, lawyer and former First Lady of the United States

Good health is the foundation of a good life, but for many of us, it's challenging to have and maintain a healthy body. We can change some things—such as diet, alcohol consumption, and exercise—but other things—like osteoarthritis, cataracts, and even some cancers—are part of the aging process.

You've heard it before and perhaps you know it from firsthand experience: growing old is no fun at all. There's no way around the fact that losing some of our physical abilities just plain sucks. While some of the challenges to our bodies are unavoidable, others are clearly our own fault. Your inner track star or cheerleader is now a distant memory, and because you've stopped using your body, it's easy to believe you've permanently lost it. If that's how you think, you're simply fooling yourself into believing a myth. Even if you've been sedentary for years, you can do something about it. It means taking baby steps at first, but eventually— if you get out of your own way—your body will choose health.

In assessing your physical health, you might want to think about your lifestyle. Can you do most of the things you want to do, or are you limited in some way that is out of your control? If you lost the fifty pounds your doctor has been nagging you about for the past ten years, would it make a difference? Are you getting enough sleep and drinking enough water? What about the long-overdue knee or hip replacement? What's stopping you?

If you were born with a physical defect such as a bad heart or have a genetic propensity for high cholesterol or diabetes, what's the reality of your situation? Are you using poor health as an excuse, or are you doing what you want in spite of your circumstances or limitations?

Now for the moment of truth. Rate the following statements:

My physical health is good. I can do just about anything and everything I want to do.

1	2	3	4	5	6	7	8	9	10

Although I have some limitations due to a chronic health condition, I know how to work around them.

1	2	3	4	5	6	7	8	9	10

Fitness is an important part of my life and I exercise regularly.

1	2	3	4	5	6	7	8	9	10

I eat healthy, natural foods.

1	2	3	4	5	6	7	8	9	10

I do not drink more alcohol than I should.

1	2	3	4	5	6	7	8	9	10

I do not smoke.

1	2	3	4	5	6	7	8	9	10

If you've just come back from hiking Machu Picchu, congratulations—you're a force to be reckoned with, and you can use the information in this chapter to inspire a friend.

If your physical health really is beyond your control, odds are you've been dealing with those issues for a long time and we commend you for your stamina and coping skills. If you are constantly complaining about aches and pains and yet another failed attempt at losing weight, we have some ideas that just might change your life in a positive way. Finally, if you're willing to take charge of your health, we applaud your attitude. You'll find an abundance of good ideas right here.

DEFINING PHYSICAL WELLNESS

What, exactly, do we mean by physical wellness? We like this definition: "The physical dimension of wellness encourages cardiovascular flexibility and strength and also encourages regular physical activity. Physical development encourages knowledge about food and nutrition and discourages the use of tobacco, drugs, and excessive alcohol consumption. Physical wellness encourages consumption and activities that contribute to high-level wellness, including medical self-care and appropriate use of the medical system." [1]

Before we go any further, let's discuss the obvious: the things you know are bad for you that you keep doing anyway—like smoking, regularly eating fast food, drinking too much alcohol, overeating, loading up on sodium, yo-yo dieting, and lying to yourself about how you feel. You're not the only one who's hurt by this kind of self-sabotage. If your irresponsible behavior requires masses of meds to combat the resulting problems, you don't get to complain about how much you're paying for drugs. Sure, that sounds harsh, but your lack of responsibility for your well-being leads to rising insurance premiums for everyone else, and that's just not right.

When was the last time you had a checkup? Mammogram? Pap smear? Scan for skin cancer? Blood test? Did your doctor mention anything about your cholesterol or blood pressure? Did she suggest you start exercising or lose the pounds you gained since your last visit? Did you follow her advice or did you nod in agreement, promise you'd be good, and stop for a Big Mac on the way home? Really, ladies? Who do you think you're fooling? We know it's hard to change your evil ways, but if you want to make the most of the rest of your life, you need to take some action.

Since we've mentioned the dreaded Big Mac, let's talk a little bit about the term "diet." To diet does not mean eliminating everything you love to eat until you get to your desired weight—only to gain it back (usually with a vengeance). Diet means being conscious about what and how much you put into your mouth. It's choosing food because it's fuel, not just because it tastes good. Much of the food you'll find in the grocery stores—especially boxed items located in the middle aisles—is not food at all. In spite of what the label says, it's full of sugar, preservatives, soy, saturated fats, or worse. It will make you fat and eventually it will destroy your health.

All the nutrition required to maintain a healthy body can be found in the periphery of the grocery store. Foods located in the center aisles are developed by big corporations that care about making money, not about your health. It's up to you to care about you.

Here's a simple way to make healthy food choices: Eat whole foods. If possible, eat organic fruits and vegetables, grass-fed beef, free-range chicken and poultry, and wild fish. If you're especially hungry, fill up on legumes, quinoa, and brown rice. Everything else—even whole grain bread—is a treat. And drink lots of water. A general rule to follow is this: you need as many ounces of water per day as your weight divided by two. If you're a fan of adult beverages, the Mayo Clinic recommends moderate consumption,[2] which translates to up to one drink a day for women. (Note: it is not to be served in a 20-ounce sports bottle.)

GETTING—AND STAYING—MOTIVATED

Let's pause here and think about why being healthy (or healthier) is important and make sure you have a rock-solid motive. Granted, there are some conditions that you simply have to live with, but right now we're talking about the things you can control. The desire to look and feel better must come from within. Honestly—and we're being a little tough here—if you don't care, why should anyone else?

Your friends and family might love you just the way you are, but they're not the ones suffering from indigestion, heartburn, a hiatal hernia, high blood pressure, chronic fatigue, or depression. Your husband might tell you he loves your soft caramel center, but wouldn't you rather go out dancing (kayaking, hiking, or skiing) than sit on the couch and watch another episode of "Shameless"? In our youth, our motivation might have been fitting into a pair of size 27 jeans, but now, our incentive might be more practical. It doesn't matter what it is that motivates you to take a turn toward a healthier lifestyle, just as long as it comes from within.

TAKING CONTROL OF YOUR HEALTH

All it takes is some serious determination to make the necessary shifts in your lifestyle.

Leslie changed her diet (and lost weight) when her doctor told her that if she didn't lower her cholesterol, she'd have to go on statins, something she did *not* want to do. Gretchen started walking every day to get her blood pressure down and manage stress without medication. Roxie joined a gym because she knew she'd never exercise at home.

If you don't love yourself enough to take care of your personal temple, then go ahead and do it for your grandkids, your dog, or your collection of cats. Just do it!

Arleen Hiuga

Arleen has spent the better part of her professional and personal life connecting people to quality outdoor experiences. She worked at REI for almost thirty-nine years, thirty of which were in the role of store manager.

In that capacity, Arleen helped thousands of customers improve their outdoor experiences through friendly, knowledgeable advice and appropriate outfitting. She took her role a step further and made sure that her employees found ways to merge their love of the outdoors with a career that could assist others. She was also a retail operations manager for REI, developing future leaders for the company by sharing her knowledge and commitment on a broader level.

In her personal life, Arleen served on the board of directors for the Washington State Ski and Snowboard Industries and was a citizen representative on the Washington State Parks Strategic Planning Team. For twelve years, she was a member of the board of directors of Outdoors for All Foundation, a nonprofit that enriches the lives of adults and children with disabilities by opening avenues for them to enjoy outdoor recreation.

Given Arleen's experience and expertise, she seemed to be the ideal source for information on what motivates women to get out there and move. See if you recognize yourself in any of these types—or perhaps find inspiration in one or two that resonate for you.

The Fitness Buff. Given the growing popularity of fitness trackers, more and more women are trying to get in their 10,000 steps a day. Spending time indoors isn't going to cut it—no matter how many times you go up and down the stairs or from room to room. The best way to get those steps to add up is by heading outside, whether it's for a walk around the block or a hike in the woods.

The Fresh Air Enthusiast. Anyone who has spent time out of doors knows that you feel better after exercising outside. Arleen directed us to Shinrin-yoku. org, a website that supports this belief. Shinrin-yoku is a Japanese term that means "forest bathing." The concept, which took root in the 1980s and has become a cornerstone of preventive healthcare and healing in Japanese medicine, is elegant in its simplicity: "If a person simply visits a natural area and walks in a relaxed way, there are calming, rejuvenating, and restorative benefits to be achieved."

The Social Butterfly. Exercising together with friends and family is a great way to build lasting memories of good times. Whether it's cross-country skiing through a meadow, a brisk swim in a mountain lake, or a walk on the beach, the air and the company will do you a world of good. And if you happen to be on your own, pursuing an outdoor activity just might put you in touch with new, like-minded friends.

The Follower of Tradition. Were you raised in a household that revered nature? Were camping and hiking a big part of your childhood? If so, a love of the outdoors is in your DNA. Odds are, those frequent family outings continue to bring a smile to your face and will likely lead to the following trait.

The Role Model. If you grew up spending time outdoors, you have probably encouraged that lifestyle in your own kids—who, in turn, will teach it to their children. What a fabulous family legacy!

The Competitor. Some women love testing themselves against others in competitive events—from walks and runs to golf and tennis. Constantly striving to improve your ability—within reason, of course—is an ideal way to keep your body fit and flexible.

The Non-Competitor. It isn't always necessary to beat someone else. Many women enjoy more individualized outdoor activities where they can set their own pace. This can translate to walking in the park, working in the garden, or going for a swim.

The Spiritualist. Mary Anderson, the co-founder of REI, lived to be 107. Arleen shares this story about the spiritual enrichment that Mary found in outdoor adventures.

Shortly after moving into her assisted-living home, Mary was having dinner with some of the other residents when the subject of religion came up. As they all shared their affiliations, one of them asked Mary what church she attended. Mary replied simply, "The mountains are my cathedral"—a comment that rendered her tablemates speechless. Many people, like Mary, seek—and find—inspiration and peace in nature.

The Money Saver. Outdoor exercise is free and accessible to everyone. If you want to get in shape or stay that way, all you have to do is move and breathe.

The Fun Seeker. There's no denying it: learning a new sport is fun at any age. No, you're probably not going to become a freestyle snowboarder at 65—or are you?—but you might want to try bike riding, kayaking, fishing, badminton, croquet, volleyball, or tai chi.

The Environmentalist. Spending time out of doors doesn't always involve a sport. Additional options include birdwatching; gathering mushrooms, berries, and other natural products (as long as you do the necessary research to find out what's safe to eat); viewing wildlife, wildflowers, and vegetation; or simply taking in the scenery.

The Photographer. If you enjoy being behind the lens, there are endless opportunities to put your skills to the test in the great outdoors. From birds to flowers...from critters to landscapes...nature offers up some extraordinary subject matter.

The Volunteer. When the spirit of volunteerism takes hold of you, it's time to step outside. Giving back to your community can take the shape of work in a national or state park, such as trail repair, habitat restoration, and invasive plant removal. You can also volunteer to help plant and maintain a community garden, clean up local beaches, or offer dog-walking services to those in need of help.

The Artist. There's no better inspiration than Mother Nature for the aspiring—or skilled—artist. Grab your paints, brushes, palette, and canvas, and get out there and immortalize the beauty that surrounds you.

The Traveler. Different parts of the U.S. and different parts of the world offer up their own brand of flora and fauna. Traveling beyond your immediate area promises the experience of true global outdoor diversity.

Arleen tells us that several commonalities exist among women who are physically active.

"In general, women who are active have a spirit of adventure, are open to trying something new, and are confident in themselves and in their choices. They are generally independent—or they find enough inner trust to get the help they need to take on the activities that intrigue them."

To be sure, a lot of active older women have been that way all their lives. They were involved in sports before the advent of Title IX, they were the only girls to go off the high dive at the community pool, they were the first to sign up for the company softball team, and they could always be found on the slopes during the winter months. But what about the over-fifty woman who's never been physical before?

Says Arleen, "The biggest obstacle might be her own definition of being over fifty and what that means to her. If she sees herself as limited, she will be. But if she sees herself as capable, there are numerous opportunities for her to try something new. Many nonprofit groups are open to helping women get started outdoors—Mountaineers [3], Mazamas [4], and the Sierra Club [5] are a few examples. In fact, she doesn't have to look much further than Facebook to find groups that are open to sharing information. What's more, numerous guidebooks are available to help with instruction, gear, maps, and what to expect from a particular activity."

What is your compelling reason to become a healthier person? Write it down and put it where you'll see it—on the bathroom mirror, on the dashboard of your car, on the fridge. If you can't answer that question or don't know how to make these changes on your own, please get some help. There are support groups for every imaginable issue and diagnosis. Find one and go.

DEALING WITH SERIOUS ILLNESS

If you are avoiding a visit to the doctor because you suspect you might have a serious illness, ignoring your symptoms isn't going to make them disappear. We have all been guilty of denial at one time or another, but why play roulette with your health? Many conditions that were once untreatable (HIV, AIDS, HEP C, and many types of cancer) now have an excellent prognosis, but if you don't find out what's wrong, you could sadly end up like Ramona.

Ramona had just retired from a long and successful career as a social worker. She had been experiencing a mild pain in her side for months, and mentioned it to her brother, a forensic pathologist, at Thanksgiving dinner. He encouraged her to see a doctor, and although she knew he was right, she kept putting it off. Shortly after Christmas, she suffered a stroke that turned out to be caused by pancreatic cancer. She died a week later. Preventable? Perhaps not, but by burying her head in the sand, Ramona lost any chance to extend her life and enjoy more of her well-earned retirement.

HEEDING THE INNER VOICE

When commissioned to videotape a conference designed for women with cancer, Marianne braced herself for what she expected to be a sad and somewhat depressing event. Much to her amazement, the women in attendance universally exhibited a positive attitude and remarkable resiliency. Many even expressed the belief that "cancer was the best thing that ever happened to me." *How in the world could such a serious diagnosis be the best thing*, she thought? It just didn't make sense.

As the women shared their stories with Marianne, the meaning behind the statement became clear. A potentially terminal diagnosis was the wakeup call many of them required to make the changes they knew in their hearts should have been made years before. What better motivator than the diagnosis of a potentially deadly disease? With time no longer on their side, what was there to lose?

It's unfortunate that it often takes something as dramatic as a cancer diagnosis to wake us up, to get us to pay attention to that whisper—the small, quiet voice that starts deep in the soul—that's been put aside while we've been raising kids, taking care of aging parents, babysitting grandkids, working, performing relationship triage, and distracting ourselves with thousands of other tasks until the whisper becomes a scream for us to *pay attention*. We're suddenly reminded to nurture our inner child, to be kind and loving to ourselves, and to take care of our health.

We are all here on this earth to fulfill a destiny—whether large or small. While some of us listen, many of us have spent a lifetime telling that little voice to shut up. And then we get a diagnosis, or our life partner or a child dies, and we are catapulted out of the fog into the light where we are raw and vulnerable and forced to do something.

Of course, there's no need to wait until your world comes crashing down. Instead, you can begin to pay attention. It's not essential to act immediately, but the key is to acknowledge the voice, to hear the message, and to ponder the meaning it holds for you in your present life.

Whether you want to admit it or not, you know what that voice is saying. If you don't deal with it, the result will likely be a whole lot of stress, and that will eventually take a toll on your health.

For Julie, it's a difficult conversation with her grown son about his anger issues and drug use. Pam needs to tell her daughter that she no longer wants to be the on-call, available-at-the-drop-of-a-hat babysitter. Audrey doesn't sleep because her husband's snoring keeps her up. Although the doctor recommended separate bedrooms, she would rather risk her own health than address the issue she's been dealing with for forty years. Annie's twenty-five-year marriage has disintegrated into obligation. She longs for the intimacy that died long ago, but instead of leaving, she complains to her friends who are tired of listening.

We are not suggesting that you make a move you could possibly regret. Instead, we are suggesting that you stop whatever you are doing that keeps the voice at bay and start acknowledging it. Embrace what you hear and come up with a plan.

ADJUSTING YOUR ATTITUDE

So...what's your overall attitude about physical wellness? Are you grateful for the health you do have—even when your joints ache from osteoarthritis or Lyme disease—or are you miserable and constantly complaining? Guess what? No one wants to be around the latter. When you whine and grumble, others dread helping you and don't want to be around you. But they're too nice to say it. Fortunately, we're here to give you the straight scoop.

Starting immediately, do everyone a favor and begin each day by appreciating whatever you can, whenever you can. The sun streaming through your bedroom window. Birdsong. A perfectly cooked egg for breakfast. Waffles. A smile from the mailman. A kind word from your neighbor. Music. A phone call from an old friend.

A positive attitude will attract friends and family to you, and that will cheer you up. Eventually you may actually feel better—maybe without doing anything at all. Imagine that!

If, by chance, you are one of the 100 million Americans (11.2 percent of the population) suffering from chronic pain,[6] we feel for your situation and encourage you to consider options other than opioids. From hypnosis to massage—from acupuncture to medical marijuana—there are options worth exploring that can ultimately provide pain management and a better quality of life. Talk to your doctor, get a referral to a pain management clinic or specialist, and research the topic on your own. You might have to incur some out-of-pocket expenses, and we hope you love yourself enough to make an investment in your body.

We know change is hard, but it's often necessary if you want to improve your physical health and well-being. We've made some suggestions below to help get you started. As soon as you decide on one action step, pick up the phone, make an appointment, and mark it on your calendar. Don't think about it; just do it. Then keep the appointment.

We are big fans of rewarding ourselves for effort and for our accomplishments. Rewards don't have to cost a lot—or anything at all, for that matter. Our suggestions for a "well done, you!" include: sleeping in, spending an extra hour reading a mystery, saying no when asked to do something you really don't want to do, downloading a new book onto your tablet, getting a manicure or pedicure, checking out the Silver Sneakers class at your local gym (it just might be covered by your supplemental health plan), taking yourself to a matinee, asking your partner to make dinner every Tuesday. You get the idea. Congratulations!

ACTION STEPS

I am willing to improve my physical wellness by taking the following action. (Check all that apply.)

I will reach and maintain a healthy weight. If I don't know how to do that on my own, I'll get help.

If I have physical symptoms of anything out of the ordinary, I will consult a medical professional.

I will visit my primary care physician, gynecologist, and dermatologist for an annual exam.

If I'm not used to exercising, I will start with gentle physical activity—walking, beginners' yoga, Pilates, or tai chi.

If my fitness level is high, I will run, lift weights, dance, take spin classes, or engage in some sort of high-energy activity.

I will make sure my alcohol consumption is within recommended limits.

Chapter 2

Emotional Rescue

*"Health is a state of complete physical, mental, and social
well-being, and not merely the absence of disease or infirmity."*
—World Health Organization

Although it's not often talked about, just about everyone has suffered from some type of mental health issue at one time or another. According to a recent study, "Depression affects more than 19 million Americans every year.... While depression is not a normal part of the aging process, there is a strong likelihood of it occurring when other physical health conditions are present."[7]

It wasn't so long ago that depression, anxiety, and similar disorders were not talked about. (Think about all the women with post-partum depression who suffered in silence.) Today, however, mental health issues are openly addressed. A quick internet search reveals twenty-seven celebrities who have spoken out about coping with depression and bipolar disorder, including Ellen DeGeneres, Lady Gaga, and Angelina Jolie. If you have emotional or mental health issues, you're in very lofty company.

Whether you've been a long-time sufferer with a clinical diagnosis or have had occasional bouts of depression that are mostly situational, it is not likely to be a state of mind that you would choose. On the less severe end of the spectrum are general dissatisfaction, frustration, regret, and unhappiness with some aspects of your life. Such feelings and emotions get in the way of the enjoyment, relaxation, and contentment you know you deserve.

So, how bad is it? Rate the following statements.

I am basically a happy and productive person.

1	2	3	4	5	6	7	8	9	10

When I have problems, I ask for help from a trusted friend.

1	2	3	4	5	6	7	8	9	10

When I am depressed or anxious, I am willing to talk about it.

1	2	3	4	5	6	7	8	9	10

If negative emotions get the best of me for more than a month or so, I seek professional help from a therapist.

1	2	3	4	5	6	7	8	9	10

I make an effort to spend time with people who have a positive outlook on life, because I know it's contagious.

1	2	3	4	5	6	7	8	9	10

I look forward to the future and all it might offer me.

1	2	3	4	5	6	7	8	9	10

If you are generally and genuinely optimistic and are seldom slowed down by life's little tests, you are a rare breed. If, however, you are one of the 43.8 million adults in the United States who experiences mental illness in a given year[8] and are too depressed, anxious, or manic to deal with it on your own, we strongly suggest that you get professional help. See your primary care physician, get a referral to a psychologist or psychiatrist, and get the treatment and/or medication you need to get back on track.

ACCEPTING RESPONSIBILITY

Since we're not mental health professionals, we're going to focus on the emotional issues that do not have a clinical diagnosis. In too many instances, we sabotage our happiness because we are looking outside of ourselves for salvation, expecting someone or something else to provide it. Let's make one thing clear: you are the only one who is responsible for your peace of mind, satisfaction, and contentment. How you choose to respond to the challenges that life presents is completely within your power.

Yes, that's a tough order, especially if you've been in the habit of blaming others for the way things are. But if you grasp only this one concept, it will alter your perspective and encourage you to make the necessary changes when things are not to your liking. You are not the victim, even if you might have perfected that role. As soon as you're tempted to complain about [fill in the blank], it's a message to you to respond—not react—in some appropriate way.

Claudia is a freelance graphic designer. She has a handful of clients for whom she does regular work, and although her husband's income allows the family to live comfortably, she enjoys the financial cushion that her work affords.

Frequently, friends will ask Claudia to design a logo, a flier, or a website. There is rarely an offer to pay for these services, and the assumption seems to be that she is willing to work for free since she "doesn't need the money." Because Claudia hates confrontation, she takes on these projects—and then complains bitterly to her husband: the time it takes, the frequent revisions, the push to meet unrealistic deadlines. All of these things are a never-ending source of frustration, and Claudia finally decided to take a stand.

The next time she was asked to do a *pro bono* job, she pleasantly explained that she would provide one hour of free work, and then bill the rest of her time at a special friends-and-family rate. It came as no surprise that many of these projects suddenly weren't so important to the freebie-seeker. In the instances where people were happy to be offered a reduced fee, the work was a pleasure for Claudia because she didn't feel used and abused. By setting limits, she created a win-win situation for all concerned.

Examples of responding instead of reacting include creating boundaries; saying yes only when you really mean it; saying no when you don't have the time, energy, or desire; collecting more information before you answer a question or make a commitment; being upfront about your needs, wants, and aspirations; and remaining calm.

Inappropriate ways block communication and make it difficult to enjoy the company of others. Judging, criticizing, arguing, lecturing, threatening, name-calling, and probing make us defensive and create an unpleasant atmosphere. Whether you're the recipient of this type of behavior or you're dishing it out, the result is not likely to bring you the peace and harmony you desire.

Why, then, do we behave this way? At some point in time, we have probably all been guilty of these communication *faux pas*. It's our belief that we are conditioned by our past, and when we're triggered by a comment or an event, we simply react without thinking. It goes something like this:

Your daughter asks for a $5,000 loan to pay off her credit card, and you immediately berate her for reckless and irresponsible spending. Your son asks to borrow your car because his is in the shop, and you admonish him for poor planning. Your husband gets home late from his Saturday golf game, and you're fuming because now you'll be late for your dinner reservations. Life is full of annoying little (and big) triggers, and if we let them get to us, we will never be as happy as we could be. What's a woman to do?

Let's take a look at what those triggers are and how you can deal with them the next time they come up. What are the situations that make you roll your eyes, hold your breath, stifle a scream, feel butterflies in your stomach, or want to set the house on fire and run for the hills? Write them down.

If you're having trouble making a list, you might find something that resonates among our favorites: being in the grocery checkout line behind the moron who can't find her debit card; unconscious drivers who cut us off, drive too slow, drive too fast, or text; neighbors who don't clean up after their dogs; incessantly barking dogs; telephone solicitors; sales people who aren't helpful enough; sales people who are too helpful; you-know-who's socks in the middle of the bedroom floor; wet towels on the bathroom floor; dirty dishes in the sink—the list goes on and on. We all have daily occurrences that drive us crazy and block the joy and inner peace we should be experiencing.

Rather than resign yourself to being miserable, you can choose how you react. It's that simple. For example, humor has a magical way of breaking through just about every irritation. Instead of fuming and foaming, try laughing at the things that drive you crazy. If you prefer to be more serious, simply breathe until you calm down, take some time to think, and rant in a journal where no one has to be the target of your wrath.

Go back to your list for each trigger and add an option that might make the situation more palatable and less stressful. Perhaps the next time it occurs, you'll be able to manage it without coming unglued.

CREATING YOUR OWN HAPPINESS

Having a good attitude about whatever is going on is another way to be a happier person. You don't have to like a particular situation, but it's helpful to attempt to accept what is. As we age, all sorts of issues will arise, and if we can't maintain a sense of balance and equilibrium, we are destined for a bumpy ride. Situations can be sad and depressing, but that does not mean we have to feel that way.

Stacy's husband, Jeff, was sixty-three when he was diagnosed with multiple myeloma and given a prognosis of four years. After dealing with the shock of his illness and taking some time to grieve, the two vowed to maintain as positive an outlook as possible.

Jeff continued to work at his accounting firm whenever he felt strong enough, and he also made sure that he and Stacy took plenty of time to travel and do the things they loved. It's been seven years since his diagnosis, and every day is a celebration of beating the odds.

While they know there will be bad days—while they know Jeff probably won't live to a ripe old age—they consider each day together to be a gift.

In cases like this, attitude is everything. It's also a choice. Jeff and Stacy could have been miserable and upset, but instead, they have opted to take the high road and make the most of the time they have together.

Attitude really is everything. We are all on this planet for a limited time. When and how we leave are the only variables, and as much as we'd like to believe that we have control over our destiny, the truth is that we do not. We can do things to extend our lives and to make the absolute most of the time we have, but that's about it. Living well is an inside job, and we have control over most of our thoughts and actions. So why not enjoy the good feeling we get from making positive choices?

For those of you who have not yet figured this out, the quality of your life is not about the things you possess. If it were, the dysfunction of so many Hollywood celebrities would not be in the headlines. Our culture teaches us to desire more stuff, but what we are truly seeking is a feeling of fulfillment. We want love, intimacy, friendship, understanding, and compassion. We want to be appreciated and acknowledged for our efforts. We want to be successful—however that might be defined—and to live a life that is memorable and has meaning, at least to us.

Some people have all that, but many don't. The ones who lack a sense of fulfillment try to make up for it by amassing *things*. The problem is that material possessions cannot fill an empty space inside, and—surprise!—neither can the people you hold near and dear. No matter how fabulous they are, your spouse, kids, friends, cousins, aunts, uncles, and co-workers will never, ever be able to completely prevent the feelings of emptiness that lead to unhappiness. Nor should they. Filling you up—creating a life that is balanced and joyful—is completely your responsibility.

If you are living your life on autopilot and are suddenly faced with retirement, a health issue, or an emergency that disrupts your supremely unconscious existence, you will be knocked off center. Without the customary equilibrium—without a great sense of humor or tremendous insight into human nature—you are quite likely to fall into a funk. Challenges like these are an inevitable part of life, and unless you are prepared to deal with them, they could easily consume you and take you in a direction you never imagined you would go.

There are many ways to rise to a challenge, and it may take some practice before you get it quite right. For starters, it's essential to face reality. Pretending that a situation is something it's not is an exercise in futility. Embrace a willingness to look at your life honestly and openly, take a slow and steady approach to whatever needs to be done, and be grateful for the good things.

Your thoughts and beliefs have an enormous amount of power over your joy and happiness. If, for example, you believe that your golden years will be the best you've ever had, it just might turn out that way. But if you fear ending up in a nursing home because your kids won't be able to—or won't want to—take care of you, that apprehension could lead to the reality you hope to avoid.

(Just a little aside here: if you're expecting something from your kids, we encourage you to let that thought go. Taking care of you in your old age is not their job. Of course, if they choose to help you or invite you into their home—and you want to be there—that's another thing, but expecting it will only lead to disappointment.)

It is not uncommon for fearful thoughts to become more prevalent as we get older. We spend time worrying about what happened, what is happening, and what might happen. Yes, it's true that at some point in the future you might be too old and frail to care for yourself. You might break a hip, develop a serious disease, need to downsize before you're ready, or ask your kids for financial assistance because you never in your wildest dreams thought you'd make it to ninety-five.

But what good does it do to fret about those possibilities now? It's one thing to plan for the future and another to obsess about situations that might never occur. Negative thoughts—worry, fear, and unnecessary concern—about anything can only sabotage your desire to be happy. With work and raising a family behind you, or almost behind you, wouldn't it be more productive to come up with creative ways to enjoy the day rather than worrying about it?

Review your list of the things that make you happy. Make time to do as many of those things as you can every day.

That brings us to the topic of what to do with an abundance of extra time. It's likely that you have more free hours in your life than ever before, and that can be a source of freedom and adventure—or a source of extreme anxiety. Free time can spur you on to cleaning out closets, organizing boxes of old photos, or completing the quilt that's been sitting in the sewing room for the past ten years. On the other end of the continuum, it can cause intrusive thoughts about the value and meaning of your life, making you wonder if you've done enough.

In a perpetual search for significance, questioning your worth as a human being is a common emotional trap. Even though society acknowledges and rewards actions and outcomes, it's important to remember that you are a human being, not a human doing. The only judgment day is the one in your head.

If it makes you feel better about your life, make a list of all the great things you've done for your friends and family, your community, and yourself. Yes—reading self-help books counts, and so does lowering your cholesterol by changing your diet. We often think we have to do something wildly magnanimous for it to count, when in reality, the meaning in life comes simply from the times we were kind and loving to ourselves and to others.

There is no shortage of ways in which we women sabotage our state of mind. We look in the mirror and see wrinkles that weren't there forty years ago—heck, they weren't there forty days ago!—and we beat ourselves up for aging. We stand on the scale and wonder what happened to the petite young thing who looked so hot in a bikini, and we feel enormously guilty for that second helping of chocolate mousse. We forget someone's name, or the title of a movie we just saw, or the location of a restaurant that we enjoyed just last week, and we berate ourselves for being so scatterbrained.

We try to be who we used to be or who we think we should be, and the realization that we've changed comes as a shock. Suddenly, we are swimming in thoughts that are counter-productive and lead us away from well-earned feelings of joy and happiness. It doesn't have to be this way. We can learn to be more accepting of ourselves and others. We can let go of grudges and the need to be right, and forgive people who have hurt us. We can make the decision to overcome our programming and reframe our history if we choose.

THE BODY-MIND CONNECTION

According to Linda Marie, RN, BSN, and PhD candidate in integrative medicine, "It's next to impossible to separate physical health from emotional well-being—especially as we age."

Linda has dedicated her life to working with second-half-of-life folks (yes, that's us). She is also part of this population, so she can relate to the issues we face. Linda would be the first to point out that the body, mind, and human spirit are all connected. This belief is the foundation of integrative medicine.

What this means is that illness, injury, and chronic pain—or for some of us, simply slowing down—can affect our emotional health. Without intervention, we can end up in a vicious cycle that negatively affects all aspects of life. Frustration, anxiety, anger, and other unhealthy habits can take over and become the norm.

Explains Linda, "In general, our health—both physical and emotional—is tied to the choices we make about how to think, what to eat, how to move, what to do, and the company we keep. A large part of our lifestyle is under our control. We just need to educate ourselves about what is best for us given our age, abilities, and circumstances. Everyone can choose to make health a regular habit."

At this stage of life, regardless of the past, it's possible to step into your best self without shame or guilt or any of the emotions that have previously held you back. Following are a few tools—in no particular order—to help you create a mental state that will serve you well on your journey to make the most of the rest of your life.

Exercise—We've talked about the importance of moving your body, and we can't emphasize it enough. Exercise is an important component of mental health, because it gets your endorphins flowing and is a very effective stress-reducer. If you do nothing else, walk every day. Download a step-counting app onto your phone—and use it. You'll be surprised at how many steps add up during the course of a typical day.

A 2015 study done by the University of Cambridge tracked more than 334,000 people and discovered that "a markedly reduced [health] hazard was observed between those categorized as inactive and those categorized as moderately inactive." Making the shift from no exercise at all to walking briskly for twenty minutes a day generated a "20-30 percent reduction in overall mortality risk."[9]

Meditate—You don't have to be a monk or a practicing Buddhist to make it a part of your life. According to an article in *Psychology Today*,[10] "Research shows meditation boosts your health, happiness, and success." Need more? It also enhances your social life, improves your self-control, alters your brain for the better, increases your productivity, gives you perspective, and keeps you real. That's a pretty good deal for a practice that takes little time and costs nothing.

Breathe—An article on WebMD[11] states, "Deep breathing is one of the best ways to lower stress in the body." The site recommends belly breathing for first-timers, and we agree that it's an easy way to start. Here's how:

> Sit or lie flat in a comfortable position.
>
> Place one hand on your belly just below your ribs and the other hand on your chest.
>
> Take a deep breath in through your nose and let your belly push your hand out. Your chest should not move.
>
> Breathe out through pursed lips as if you were whistling. Feel the hand on your belly go in, and use it to push all the air out.
>
> Do this breathing three to ten times. Take your time with each breath.
>
> Notice how you feel at the end of the exercise.

Speak Your Truth—You might be in the habit of keeping your mouth firmly shut when you really must speak out and say what needs to be said. Getting whatever it is off your chest can be extremely cathartic, so we highly recommend it. If possible, do it in a kind and gentle way that doesn't cause massive waves or unnecessary emotional pain.

Examine Your Fears—Many times the things you fear are imagined. You fear the unknown, and that keeps you locked into a routine. You fear people and places you read about in the news, so you refuse to travel. You fear you won't have enough money to buy the things you want and need, and that makes you hoard what you do have. You fear that your partner will leave you, so you go into smother mode. You fear that retirement will be boring, yet you do nothing to make it the exciting and rewarding time it could be. You get the idea. Look at the things you fear and decide if they are valid. Consider the odds before you cling to a belief that does not serve you.

Investigate Your Stressors—Adult kids who refuse to launch, lack of funds to do the things you want to do, illness (yours or a loved one's), a garage full of boxes that belonged to your deceased parents—all of these can generate stress. Make a list of everything that makes you crazy and figure out a way to give it less impact. Brainstorm with a girlfriend, make an appointment to see a therapist, or give hypnotherapy a shot.

Be Mindful of the Company You Keep—If you spend time around people who are chronic complainers and naysayers, it's harder to maintain a good attitude and positive outlook. Try to focus your social life on people who make you smile and laugh, and don't take yourself too seriously.

Do More Than Try—"To try" implies that you'll give something a half-hearted attempt, and if it doesn't work out, you'll convince yourself that it can't be done. It applies to tasks like losing weight, being nicer, arriving on time, saving money, having more fun, learning Spanish, and being happy—all with varying degrees of success. The next time the word "try" slips off your tongue, replace it with the word "will." "Will" holds us accountable and spurs us on.

Plan—If you're the sort of person who thrives on spontaneity, we don't want to get in the way of something that works for you. But if you're one of those people who talks about all the things you want to do—but you never actually do them—we suggest you do some research, get out your calendar, and make a plan. We're not talking about getting so hung up on the details that you become overwhelmed, but we are suggesting that you take the time required to turn at least some of your dreams into realities.

Put Your Feelings on Paper—For many people, writing is therapeutic. Journaling is a great way to process moods and opinions that aren't quite clear. It's a place to rant about things you can't or won't change. It's a way to see what's going on beneath the surface. If you just write and let the words flow, you might succeed in tapping into your subconscious and unearthing your deepest thoughts and feelings. If you're still harboring anger and resentment toward a boss or an old love who did you wrong, write a letter and tell them off. (Just don't mail it, okay?)

Stop Complaining—If you have a problem, or if an aspect of your life isn't going the way you'd like, do something other than whine about it. Initially, you might have the sympathetic ear of your family or friends, but eventually they'll stop listening. Be especially cautious of complaining about your aches and pains and how you look and feel, especially if the word "old" is part of the complaint. The antidote to feeling old is moving your body. The antidote to looking old is in Chapter 6.

Anita Jhunjhunwala Mukherjee, EdD

Born and raised in a patriarchal Indian society, Dr. Mukherjee strived from an early age to find her identity beyond predefined gender roles. She attended the Indian Institute of Science, Bangalore, to become a computer engineer, then earned her master's degree at Iowa State University. Her experience in the software industry spans many years and several different countries. While volunteering with at-risk populations, she opted to complete a doctorate in counseling psychology so she could focus on mental health and quality of life. She currently works as a licensed psychologist and is the author of Asian Indian Older Adults in Silicon Valley: Quality of life of parents who immigrate to reunite with their children. *Here she shares her expertise on emotional issues in women over fifty.*

AUTHORS: *Given your background in engineering and your career shift to psychology, how can you best describe the difference between science and psychology?*

DR. MUKHERJEE: In the realm of science, if A + B = C, that will always be the case, forever and ever. In psychology, a single, constant answer does not apply to all. Different individuals and different circumstances will yield different outcomes. In the case of divorce, for example, the people and the context vary, so the emotional impact could be positive for some and negative for others.

AUTHORS: *In your experience, what are the most common emotional and mental health issues in women over fifty?*

DR. MUKHERJEE: That really depends on the particular life situation. As women age, they experience different types of losses: the failing health of self or others, career issues. Their relationships also change—with partners, children, parents, and others—and if any relationship is not going well, that becomes a significant stressor. Regardless of the cause of the stress, the problem can manifest as depression, anxiety, substance abuse, or a midlife crisis, although the latter is less common than you might expect.

Issues for older women can also be partially triggered by ageism. As a whole, society in the United States often treats the aging population as disposable or as a burden. Other cultures respect their elders, which is what I experienced growing up in India. Family bonds were strong there, and the connectivity among generations was a way of life—although I must admit that the situation has changed significantly in recent years over there, too.

AUTHORS: *Let's talk about aging. Is it a downhill ride?*

DR. MUKHERJEE: It's a common perception that aging is a process of linear, progressive decline, but new research says that's just not true. Some things decline with age, but other things stay the same while still others improve. In particular, emotional health actually improves. Barring extenuating circumstances, you can learn new things, strengthen your body, and expand your coping mechanisms at any age.

AUTHORS: *What are the options for treating age-related issues in women?*

DR. MUKHERJEE: Treatment strategies are very individualized. What works for one person may not work for another. Moreover, what works one day might not work the next day, so it is important to have a toolbox of strategies to draw from. In therapy, the orientation of the therapist also matters. For example, I take a holistic approach—treating the body, mind, and spirit as an integrated whole. Simultaneously addressing all domains of a person, I think, is the most effective solution.

AUTHORS: *We fifty-plus women often joke about losing our memory. What can you tell us about dementia or Alzheimer's?*

DR. MUKHERJEE: Although people attribute memory loss only to dementia or Alzheimer's, there could be many causes. For example, depression in older adults can result in memory loss, a condition called pseudo-dementia.

One way to differentiate the two is that gradual memory loss is usually dementia, while abrupt memory loss is usually depression.

AUTHORS: *What are the symptoms of depression?*

DR. MUKHERJEE: Symptoms of depression vary with age. In younger adults, it may be a dysphoric mood, while in older adults, somatic symptoms such as aches and pains, lack of concentration, fatigue, and memory problems are common.

AUTHORS: *Is medication a good solution for depression or anxiety?*

DR. MUKHERJEE: Medication is certainly an option with or without therapy. However, you have to look at the long-term effects and also determine the cause of the problem. If you look solely at the biomedical model, which focuses on the physical or biological aspects of an illness, you can easily over-look the psychological, environmental, and social influences that might be causing or contributing to the problem. Simply fixing the biochemistry without addressing the underlying causes will not resolve the issue.

AUTHORS: *Lack of sleep is an issue for many post-menopausal women. What suggestions do you have for dealing with those endless nights?*

DR. MUKHERJEE: The inability to fall asleep and stay asleep is often due to depression or anxiety, although some people sleep more when they're depressed. You could use medicines to treat insomnia. In addition, several healthy behavioral changes, known as sleep hygiene factors, can help you sleep better. However, it is important to take into account a person's cultural back-ground when talking about sleep hygiene. For example, while an absolutely quiet environment is usually recommended, I've had clients who complain that they cannot sleep if it is too quiet. So, if you grew up sleeping to the sounds of people talking or television or city traffic, you might fall asleep better with some ambient noise that perhaps shuts off after a while.

Worrying that you cannot sleep could itself aggravate the problem, so I often suggest to my patients that they treat sleeplessness as an opportunity. Instead of lying in bed fretting over the fact that you can't fall asleep, use those wide-awake hours to do something productive or something you enjoy: read a book, finish some chores, journal, or meditate. You'll have a feeling of accom-plishment, and that may relax you enough to fall asleep.

AUTHORS: *Are there things a woman can do to stay emotionally healthy?*

DR. MUKHERJEE: One of the best things one can do is to accept change. Change is the only constant in life, and problems occur when you try to resist it. Life will always present challenges, and it's how you respond to them that truly matters. When faced with a crisis of any magnitude, you can either emerge stronger or you can break down.

Women over fifty are faced with change on a regular basis. Children leave the nest. Careers alter or cease to be. Marriages end in divorce or there is the death of parents, spouse, relatives, or friends. Because of these major transitions, it is essential to recognize and accept what cannot be changed.

Once you learn to accept life's ebbs and flows, there are other strategies you can employ to maximize your emotional health. I recommend yoga and pranayama, breath and sound exercises, and meditation. Changing your self-talk from negative to positive is another important strategy.

Also, let's not underestimate the therapeutic power of healthy relationships. It's not about how many friends you have, but about the quality of the friendships. It's about being comfortable enough to share the things that are important to you and getting the feedback you need...being able to confide in someone and knowing that your secrets will be respected.

Genetics can play a part in a woman's resiliency, but attitude is key. In the famous Nun Study, it was shown that the brain chemistry for some nuns indicated Alzheimer's, but the disease didn't manifest. So if a person has purpose and meaning in life, it's actually possible to stay healthier. Creating goals and having a sense of self-efficacy or control over goals goes a long way toward better physical and mental health.

AUTHORS: *What are your thoughts about older parents moving away from home to be closer to their adult children—either moving in with them or living nearby?*

DR. MUKHERJEE: Sometimes it works; sometimes it doesn't. If parents can make the move and continue to lead rich, full lives, that's a good thing. But if leaving behind the people and things they know and love causes feelings of loneliness and isolation, it will create serious emotional problems.

Many additional factors come into play, including the parents' physical health, culture, and relationships with their children. Do they feel wanted and needed? If not, that's depression just waiting to happen. And if they start feeling that they are not needed, then they start questioning the point of being alive.

AUTHORS: *What do you think is the biggest barrier to mental and emotional health?*

DR. MUKHEREE: Without a doubt, problems arise when you are engaged in behaviors that are not ego-syntonic—that is, not in harmony with your value system, comfort zone, and self-image. It is important to look within yourself to determine if a particular action is something you want to be doing or if it is contrary to your wishes and beliefs. Remember, you can pretend in front of the world, but you can't hide the truth from your conscience.

AUTHORS: *Is there anything else you think women fifty-plus should know about maintaining a positive attitude?*

DR. MUKHERJEE: Emotional problems often arise because people are looking for perfect solutions—all pros and no cons. In reality, most often such perfect options do not exist. So, any action you take will have both positive and negative ramifications, and your job is to weigh them to help you decide. If you dither too long and do not make a decision, that's a decision in itself.

Just remember that human nature is a quirky thing, and research shows that as soon as you decide on decision A, decision B will immediately look more attractive and vice versa. So once a decision is made, stop ruminating over it; stop blaming yourself if things don't work out. Remember that if you chose option B, current problems may have been avoided, but some new problems could have arisen.

ACTION STEPS

I am willing to improve my mental health and emotional state of being by taking the following action. (Check all that apply.)	
If I have an emotional problem that I cannot resolve, I will make an appointment to call my doctor or therapist to talk about it, and I will heed the advice I am given.	
I will examine my fears to determine whether they are real or imagined.	
I will look at the stressors in my life and come up with ways to minimize them.	
I will seek out people who are happy, joyful, and fun, and I will try to avoid situations that have a negative impact on my emotional state.	
I will quit complaining about [fill in the blank] and instead do something about it.	
I will meditate, pray, or sit quietly for at least five minutes each day.	

Chapter 3

Money Management 101

"A woman's best protection is a little money of her own."
— Clare Boothe Luce, U.S. Ambassador

By a certain age, we have either lived up to (and maybe exceeded) our financial expectations, we are floundering downstream of our dreams, or we are somewhere in the middle—short of our vision, but comfortable with our circumstances. If you're not quite where you want to be and are still in the workforce, there might be time to make up the losses you experienced during the dot-com or housing crises. For most of us, however, our financial status is what it is at this point in our lives.

Ideally, our basic expenses—food, clothing, shelter—are covered, with enough left over for some fun. In the best of all worlds, we have sufficient resources to survive well into our eighties without having to depend on our children or the kindness of others.

For many people in their fifties and sixties, the financial picture is pretty bleak. In the article "Are We in a Baby Boomer Retirement Crisis?" by Barbara A. Friedberg,[12] the writer states, "Baby boomers, born between 1946 and 1964, are heading into retirement in droves (about 10,000 *a day*, in fact). Along with the aging of this iconic cohort come lots of data about their poor preparation for the future. Insufficient preparedness and lack of financial resources for decades without steady employment paint a gloomy picture for many retirees." Depressed yet?

Gloomy or not, there are things you can do to improve your financial situation, regardless of what it is. But first, let's figure out where you stand. Because money can be such an emotionally charged issue, we want to remind you that, while it is important to have enough to care for yourself, it's not as important as health, friendship, love, and happiness. If your financial situation is stressing you out and affecting your emotional well-being, the first step is being honest about your circumstances. Here we go.

I have enough money to live well into my eighties and beyond.									
1	2	3	4	5	6	7	8	9	10

The amount of money I have going out does not exceed the amount of money I have coming in.									
1	2	3	4	5	6	7	8	9	10

I am confident that my money is being managed competently.									
1	2	3	4	5	6	7	8	9	10

I have no debt and I own my own home.									
1	2	3	4	5	6	7	8	9	10

I have enough money to leave something to my children, friends, or charities.									
1	2	3	4	5	6	7	8	9	10

I am satisfied with my ability to handle money and I am pleased with my financial situation.									
1	2	3	4	5	6	7	8	9	10

How did you fare? If you're financially solvent, pat yourself on the back and go out and have some fun. If you enjoy traveling, splurge on an around-the-world ticket and blog about your adventures. Buy that fifth wheel you've dreamed about, visit family and friends, and see America. If you're more of a homebody, give your kid the down payment for a house, donate more to charity, or boost your generosity to those less fortunate.

PUTTING YOUR FINANCIAL AFFAIRS IN ORDER

It's common knowledge that everyone who has anything should write a will, but if you have a significant amount of assets (more than $150,000) and want to avoid probate (and yes, you do), meet with a lawyer to discuss the option of putting your assets into a living trust.[13] Again, the internet is full of information on this topic, including the difference between wills and trusts. (You just might need both.) We also recommend searching the bar association website for your state to find forms that can help you with this process.

With your trust and will behind you, you might want to consider hiring a bookkeeper and/or setting up automatic bill pay for regular expenses. It's easy to pay bills on time when you're home in front of your calendar and computer, but if you plan on traveling or admit to being more forgetful than you were twenty years ago, this simple step can save you a lot of grief and move a recurring task off your plate.

As an aside, ladies, if you have relegated all the household finances to your spouse, it's time to start paying attention. As a general rule, women live five years longer than men, so odds are you might ultimately have to take on this responsibility regardless of how you feel about it. At a time when you're dealing with sadness and grief over the loss of your partner, you don't want to add financial confusion to the mix.

Once your financial affairs are in order, breathe a huge sigh of relief and do something fun that you've always wanted to do. Need help with that? You'll find it in Chapter 4.

FINDING THE HELP YOU NEED

If you're still struggling financially, don't be embarrassed or ashamed by your less-than-stellar situation. Money management is an area where many of us, especially boomers, can use some assistance. Fortunately, help is everywhere. From Debtors Anonymous to Suze Orman, there is an abundance of information to help you get back on your feet. If all else fails, get the government assistance you need to keep clothes on your back, food in your belly, and a roof over your head.

Whether you need to overcome a dire financial situation or streamline your spending, you have to do *something* to change your circumstances. You can't just sit back and hope that things will magically improve. Gone are the days when being adorable could get you a free meal, so this is in your hands.

Mary was divorced thirty years ago. Since then, she raised two children on her own, earned a master's degree in psychology, started a hypnotherapy practice, and created an environmental nonprofit. Although her work was rewarding, it was not financially sustainable. After several years of attempting to keep her business afloat, she found herself in serious need of cash. To make ends meet, she started cleaning houses.

All went relatively well until Mary contracted a virus and was unable to work. Her finances rapidly dwindled, and fear kicked in. Swallowing her pride, she asked her ex-husband for help. To her surprise, he agreed to pay off her credit card and supplement her income. Out from under her financial burden, Mary reinstated her license as a hypnotherapist, took a series of continuing education classes, and reopened her practice. Today, at seventy-six, she teaches stress-management classes, co-hosts women's groups, and sees clients twice a week. Although she is far from wealthy, she is comfortable, secure, and enjoying her life.

Mary's story is an example of how it is possible to turn your life around—if you're willing to think outside the box to come up with solutions to apparently insurmountable problems. When a situation is dire, play it out in your head to determine the worst that could happen. In Mary's case, her ex could have said no, which is clearly not the end of the world. Instead it simply means that she'd have to move on to another way to get out of her financial hole.

No one wants to be in this kind of situation, but if you find yourself there, sidestep feelings of shame and guilt, do some brainstorming, and generate a list of possible solutions. There are plenty of women who are working well into their seventies—some because they love to work, and others because they have to.

EXPLORING THE JOB MARKET

As an older worker, you might not be making top dollar, but at least you will be getting some income. With a little help from a financial planner, you might be able to create a stable financial situation—even at this time in your life. If you think there are no jobs for women of a certain age, think again. With a little bit of research and a smattering of soul-searching, you just might come up with a possibility that works for your situation.

Let's look at some self-employment options that have worked for other members of the sisterhood.

If you like kids, consider advertising your services as a granny nanny. Working moms are always looking for reliable childcare, and the website RentAGrandma.com lets you create a profile and negotiate terms directly with each family. You can also take this business opportunity to the next level, since the company offers franchises.

If cooking is your passion, market yourself as a neighborhood personal chef. Make daily batches of soups, stews, or casseroles to sell to your working neighbors, who can pick up dinner from you on their way home. (Check your state's cottage food law—which allows you to make certain types of food from your home kitchen and sell it—to be sure you can do this legally.)

If you've been knitting or crocheting for years and have a backlog of afghans, socks, hats, and scarves, put them on consignment at a local shop or sell them online at Etsy.com. You can find other web-based shops at http://moneypantry.com/etsy-alternatives.

If you love animals, start a pet-walking and/or pet-care service.

Establish yourself as a home-care professional—for a fee, of course. When your neighbors go on vacation, they can turn to reliable you to take in the mail and newspaper, water the plants, and generally keep an eye on things. Your comings and goings will also make it look like someone's home.

Have you been growing your own vegetables for years? If so, let your skills generate revenue by offering a series of classes on how to grow perfect tomatoes, greens, or herbs. If you're the neighbor with the enviable flower garden, teaching classes can work for you, too.

Maybe you're a math whiz or a word nerd. If so, offer your services as a tutor. If you're an expert in a particular field, you might also consider teaching classes at your local community college. Find out who's in charge and schedule an appointment to learn what is required and if you have the proper certification.

If you're tired of paying your mortgage or rent, housesitting might be your answer. The book *Break Free: The Ultimate Guide to Housesitting*[14] explains everything you need to get started.

The trick to being successfully self-employed is to choose something you're excited about, then get the word out to people in your community who need your services. Your marketing efforts can be as simple as fliers and word-of-mouth.

If you prefer working for someone else and receiving a regular paycheck, we direct you again to the magic of the internet. You may be happily surprised to discover that there really are jobs geared specifically to us.

moneypantry.com/extra-income-for-seniors/

USAjobs.gov—Temporary and part-time government jobs, some of which offer the added bonus of benefits

www.doleta.gov/seniors—The Department of Labor's Senior Community Service Employment Program, which offers training and help with job placement to low-income folks ages 55 and up

www.coolworks.com/older-bolder/—Seasonal jobs at national parks

encore.org/fellowships/—An opportunity to share the skills and knowledge you've spent your life acquiring via paid contracts with host organizations: six months to a year, full- or half-time positions

The idea is to be creative, do what you can, and above all, avoid feeling sorry for yourself. If you are too sick or disabled to work, then by all means call Social Services and get them to help you—even if it means food stamps, Medicaid, and/or subsidized housing.

TAKING SMART STEPS

Monitor Your Credit Report—Checking your credit report on a regular basis is the best way to protect against identity theft. You can get a free credit report once a year from the three credit-reporting agencies: Equifax, Experian, and Trans Union.

Subscribe to an Identity Theft Protection Service—Check with your bank, credit union, or the following organizations that focus exclusively on this service: IdentityForce, LifeLock, ID Watchdog, TrustedID, Identity Guard, Identity Fraud, PrivacyGuard, Identity Protect by Intelius, IDFreeze by myFICO, and ID Patrol by Equifax. Simply Google them for more information on the features they offer and how to sign up.

Think Twice before Canceling the Credit Cards You Never Use—If you're tempted to go on a wild shopping spree because you have $20,000 in credit on a card you haven't touched in years, by all means cancel it. But if you think you're going to raise your credit score by doing so, think again. According to myFICO.com, your FICO score is based on something called credit utilization ratio, which compares your used credit to your available credit. A high ratio is bad; a low ratio is good. By closing a card you seldom use, you eliminate a chunk of your available credit, increasing your ratio.

And While You're at It...

Since we're talking about essential issues and tasks, this is a good time to mention something about your last wishes. It's important to make these desires known to your family sooner rather than later, because if you don't spell things out for them, they're not going to know what to do when you leave this realm.

What type of memorial service do you want? Will there be singing and dancing or moaning and wailing? Do you want music, and if so, what kind? Classical? The rock of your youth? Do you prefer interment or cremation? Where do you want your body buried or ashes scattered? You might not care about any of this, and if that's the case, put that in writing, too. Forms abound to help with this task, and you can find an example here: state.gov/documents/organization/154946.pdf.

Talking about death makes many people uncomfortable, so putting your wishes in writing is a simple workaround that will truly help your family. It also gives you an opportunity to say things that need to be said and even write your own obituary or a letter to your kids. While you're at it, be sure you complete a durable power of attorney—a trusted friend or family member who can decide your fate if you are too incapacitated to do it for yourself.

Most of us say we don't want to be kept alive if there is no quality of life, but it's important to define "quality."

Judi Townsend

Judi is the owner of *Mannequin Madness* in California's Bay Area. Her company buys mannequins from retailers that have closed up shop or remodeled, then sells or rents them to clients for a variety of uses—from displays to props, from art to furniture. She didn't plan on making this her career. In fact, she was well established in the tech industry when she became an "accidental entrepreneur."

Explains Judi, "I was working at a dotcom in the early 2000s and making a very good income. I knew I ultimately wanted to do something more creative, but I didn't know what that might be. I'd always been intrigued by mannequins, and I fantasized about covering one with mosaic tiles and displaying it in my backyard, but that clearly had nothing to do with a creative job."

One day, while searching on Craigslist for concert tickets, Judi came across a man who was selling a mannequin. Thinking that would be a great way to get her backyard project started, she went to his place of business and discovered that he had about fifty mannequins for sale. As it turned out, he ran the only mannequin rental business in town, and he was leaving the state in a couple of weeks. As soon as Judi heard the words, she had an *aha* moment. *Given the level of creativity in the Bay Area, she thought, surely there should be at least one place in the region to rent a mannequin!*

Impulsively, she decided to buy the entire inventory. Her plan was to create a side business—something she could do while still working full time. She sold and rented mannequins for about a year and then 9/11 happened—and she lost her job.

"It was a time of such great fear," says Judi, "and it made me want to be more fearless. Instead of looking for another job, I decided to give the mannequin business a real shot."

She began to get cast-off mannequins from retail stores, and her stock grew from fifty to 500 in a very short period of time. She kept them in her backyard. Her basement. Her garage. Eventually, boxes full of mannequins lined her driveway.

Judi admits that when she was working out of her home, she didn't take things quite seriously. She didn't know many people who ran their own business, so finding direction and support was a nearly impossible task. As much as she was trying to "live fearlessly," she was still somewhat nervous about saying that the mannequins were her actual business—especially when people would ask incredulously, "You do *what* for a living?"

To compound the issue, her parents thought she was crazy—hence the name Mannequin Madness. They paid for her to go to the University of Southern California, and here she was using her degree to essentially play with dolls.

Trusting her gut and tapping into her knowledge of sales and marketing, Judi continued to move forward. Even though she had never worked in retail, she hoped to transfer her past experiences into her new business. She didn't hesitate to ask for support when she needed it, and she was quick to delegate tasks that she simply wasn't good at.

Says Judi, "I was slow to call myself an entrepreneur, because in the Bay Area, an entrepreneur is typically a youngish, techy male. There were no business owners who looked like me, which caused my confidence to ebb and flow. *Can I really do this? Am I crazy?* Not having any role models made it difficult to see that I truly am an entrepreneur."

The turning point was when she moved her operation out of her home and into a commercial building. Suddenly, it became the real deal. Judi now works out of a 3,400-square-foot warehouse and has five employees and five independent contractors working with her. Her inventory is in the thousands—full mannequins, plus a massive assortment of legs, hands, feet, and torsos. She shares the following wisdom with our readers.

"When I started this business, I was in my late forties and still in need of outside validation. Now I'm sixty, and these days I don't give a fuck—excuse my French—about what anyone else says. I think that as I've gotten older, I've become more confident in the business and less likely to care about the reactions of others.

"My advice to women is to listen to your inner voice despite what others might say. I had no idea my career was going to end up like this, but I knew I wanted to do something enjoyable and fulfilling, and I continued to feed that. Sometimes we have to stay away from the naysayers who tell us all the reasons why not—and surround ourselves with people who say *why not?*

"I'm more satisfied now than ever before. I'm in a creative field, and I'm doing something I really enjoy—not something I'm forced to do. The great thing about being on your own is that nobody tells you that you can't do something. When you're on your own, you're able to set your own path."

Judi is a firm believer in not stopping, regardless of the obstacles you think might litter your path. She's aware that we always have choices, even after we reach a certain age.

"Some sixty-year-old women are like what sixty used to be. They retire from work and retire from life, thinking they're too old to do anything. It makes me sad to see that, because it doesn't have to be that way. Then there are the women who refuse to stop. I'm part of that tribe, and I love being actively engaged in something meaningful. This segment of the sisterhood might be slower than we used to be, but we're still *doing.*"

Now armed with the information presented in this chapter, how will you proceed?

ACTION STEPS

I am willing to improve my financial situation by taking the following action. (Check all that apply.)

I will be honest with myself about my finances and, if necessary, tighten my belt in any way possible.

I will talk to a financial planner (or use an online calculator) and figure out how much money I need to live until I'm 89.

If I am able and if it is necessary, I will look for some enjoyable part-time work.

I will put my affairs in order by preparing a will, power of attorney, advanced directive, or any other necessary items.

I am willing to curtail my spending, and I will join a support group to help, if necessary.

If I need to be more knowledgeable about finances, I will take a workshop on money management. (These are often available free of charge through banks and credit unions.)

Chapter 4

Lovers and Children and Friends, Oh My!

"You never lose by loving. You always lose by holding back."
— Barbara De Angelis, American relationship consultant

If you have your health and enough money to do some of the things you love to do, the next important area to look at is the relationships you have with family, friends, and members of your community. People always come and go, but as we get older, they seem to do it at a faster pace. Suddenly, you realize that the people you once relied on are no longer there.

Your walking buddy from around the corner moved to Fort Lauderdale to be closer to her aging parents. The kids have their own friends and family, so you don't spend as much time with them as you used to. Now that you're retired, the co-workers you left behind have devolved into mere acquaintances, because they're still busy in the work force and have little time to socialize. Your spouse needs a hip replacement but refuses to have the surgery, or worse—your life partner dies suddenly.

If you've experienced the death of a loved one and are feeling depressed, please get into grief counseling. Most hospitals and hospice groups offer this type of service, and we encourage you to take advantage of it.

Many widows have told us that after the funeral or memorial service, friends stop calling. Odds are it's because they aren't comfortable dealing with death, so they don't make contact because they don't know what to say. Avoidance leads to embarrassment and guilt and the next thing you know, that couple you and your partner had so many good times with has vanished. Trust us, it's not about you. It just means you need to make some new friends.

According to Amy Banks, MD, director of advanced training at the Jean Baker Miller Training Institute at the Wellesley Centers for Women, "Neuroscience is confirming that our nervous systems want us to connect with other human beings."

Isolation and loneliness are not meant to be part of the human experience. Even if you're the ultimate introvert...even if you are convinced you're better off alone...your health depends on good relationships. That means having a handful of people in your life to talk to, confide in, laugh with, and share the inevitable ups and downs.

If the people you have always relied on are no longer close by, you just might have to hone your communication skills, put on your charm, get out of the house, and make the effort to cultivate some new friends. This might seem like a tall order, but it's a necessary one to fill. While it's tempting to depend on your partner, children, or the one or two buddies you still have, your well-being hinges on having a variety of people in your life.

Let's pause and take stock.

I live in the same area where I grew up, and I am surrounded by my adult children, their families, and friends I've known since kindergarten.

1	2	3	4	5	6	7	8	9	10

I live in a close-knit community with lots of friends and emotional support.

1	2	3	4	5	6	7	8	9	10

I have a life partner who is healthy, and we have a strong social network.

1	2	3	4	5	6	7	8	9	10

I live alone, but I am actively involved in my community/place of worship/meditation group/spiritual group.

1	2	3	4	5	6	7	8	9	10

I have many interests and hobbies, as well as people to share them with.

1	2	3	4	5	6	7	8	9	10

I seem to make new friends wherever I go.

1	2	3	4	5	6	7	8	9	10

How did you score? Are you overwhelmed with family and friends who can't get enough of you, or is it time to reach out and make some new acquaintances? In this chapter, we'll cover several ways to expand your circle—even if your social skills are a bit rusty—and find people in and around your area who are in the same position.

If you need more proof about the importance of relationships for your overall health, consider the Harvard Study of Adult Development[15] that began nearly eighty years ago. In 1938, scientists began tracking the health of 268 Harvard sophomores to understand what factors contribute to a healthy and happy life. Initially, the research included only men (since women didn't attend Harvard at that time), but 1,300 female and male offspring, now in their fifties and sixties, are currently included.

Robert Waldinger, the director of the study who is also a psychiatrist at Massachusetts General Hospital and a professor of psychiatry at Harvard Medical School, states that several surprising outcomes have been revealed:

> How happy we are in our relationships has a powerful influence on our health.

> Tending to relationships is an important aspect of self-care.

> Close relationships, more than fame or fortune, are what keep people happy.

> Regardless of social status, good relationships provide protection from life's hurdles, help delay mental and physical decline, and "are a better predictor of longevity and happiness than social class, IQ, or genetics."

Now that you know how important relationships are, it's time to make sure you have enough of them to feed your spirit. If you're striving for quality and making this phase of life as good as it can be, generating a steady influx of like-minded individuals is essential. Of course, you want to hang on to and cherish the connections that have taken you this far, but at the same time, it's important to be open to new friendships.

You will be amazed at how many opportunities exist to connect with others to do everything from ballroom dancing to hiking. Of course, it might be a tad uncomfortable to walk into a room full of strangers, but you made it through the first day of high school, and if you could do that, you can do anything.

DOING WHAT YOU LOVE

It's a sad fact that meeting new people—even doing the things you want to do—often fails to be a priority. It's easy to spend your time involved in the lives of your significant other, kids, grandkids, aging parents, and siblings. As you become absorbed in their routines, the things *you* like to do fade into the background.

How can you possibly go to Pilates if you have to take your dad to the urologist? How can you even think about volunteering at the animal shelter if your sister just found out her husband is having an affair? How can you enjoy a leisurely afternoon of shopping if your grown kid just lost his job—the third one in six months?

The truth is, you're no good to anyone else if you're not good to yourself. Putting the needs of others first will ultimately lead to deep resentment—not to mention a very empty life. So figure out what you like to do and get out there and do it. The relationships you forge during the process just might save your sanity and extend your life.

When Marcella moved to her community thirty years ago, she was a single mom who worked a full-time job and spent every weekend biking or running with friends. As the years passed, she remarried, cared for her husband when he developed ALS, ultimately lost him to the disease, had two knee replacements, and retired. The changes in her life caused changes in her friendships, and many of them fell by the wayside over the course of time.

Although Marcella is physically incapable of returning to her early love of cycling and running, that doesn't mean she's relegated to sitting at home on the couch. Recognizing the need to do something that included both people and exercise, she started exploring activities that might work for her. A tai chi class advertised on a local bulletin board caught her attention, and she decided to give it a try. Because no stress on her knees was involved, she could do the moves easily and comfortably. Before long she was taking three classes a week, connecting with other students, and spending leisure time with them outside of class.

Maybe so much time has passed that you don't even know what you enjoy or want to do. If you are like many women who were so caught up in career and family that you did little else, now might be your opportunity to pick up a hobby and meet people that way.

If the concept of a hobby is alien to you, we suggest that you visit discoverahobby.com. From salsa dancing to historical reenactments...from cooking to wine-tasting...from jewelry-making to quilting...the site lists hundreds of activities and resources to help you get started.

Once you find something that appeals to you, look for a local group that shares your interest. Meetup.com is a social networking site that helps connect users with similar pursuits. If you don't find a relevant group in your area, start one of your own.

Another way to build friendships is through traveling—and it can be as simple as a day trip. During the holiday season, many small towns offer bus trips to larger cities for shopping opportunities. This is an ideal way to accomplish your gift-buying while making new relationships around retail therapy.

Cities and towns located within an hour or two of a casino often feature daily bus trips, affording an opportunity to get to know your traveling companions before you arrive. Even if you're not into gaming, casinos are a great source of free or low-cost live entertainment and ridiculously inexpensive lunches.

If you're open to going places alone, your options expand exponentially. Many towns are home to art galleries, museums, and cultural events that you can comfortably attend alone and chat with others along the way. Or head to a local coffee house—the busier, the better—where conversations abound. If you love the outdoors, check out a nearby nature trail. By returning at the same time once or twice a week, the strangers you see will become familiar faces. If you love sports, theater, or music and you're not brave enough to buy a single ticket, consider volunteering as an usher.

Of course, longer trips can be a fantastic way to meet people who enjoy experiencing new places. If you think you can't afford it, think again. Some of our friends are tour coordinators with Go Ahead Tours,[16] which means they get airfare, meals, and accommodations for next to nothing in exchange for recruiting travelers for the company's many excursions.

If you want to travel but are nervous about doing it alone, the internet abounds with options for over-fifty single travelers. Check out backroads.com, adventures-abroad.com, women-traveling.com, and goaway.com/trips/typ/single-friendly. If you enjoy learning about various cultures, don't overlook roadscholar.org.

You might even consider joining the Peace Corps,[17] which has positions for folks age fifty-plus. Our friend Anne—who retired from teaching and working as a junior high school librarian—is in the midst of a two-year commitment in Morocco, where she teaches English classes and writes grants for local projects.

We understand that not everyone is comfortable making conversation with a stranger, but it's a lot easier than it was in high school. To get started, try asking a question. Let's say you decide to check out the local walking meet-up, and you notice a woman wearing a great pair of hiking boots. That's your cue to say something like, "Those boots look really comfortable. Did you buy them here in town?" Or during the walk, you notice several flowers that are in full bloom. Horticulture isn't your thing, so you ask if anyone can identify them. Before you know it, you've launched a conversation about lupine and gardening. If you're out of practice, the key to starting a conversation is simple: make a comment, ask a question, and listen.

DEALING WITH INTIMATE RELATIONSHIPS

Your partner has lost interest in sex, but you're still in your prime.

He's on Viagra, but your libido is a thing of the past.

Your significant other has been unfaithful, and even though your body craves intimacy, your head is resisting.

You want to have sex, but it's too painful.

You're back in the dating scene and like the idea of a sex life, but you're worried about herpes and AIDS.

As disparate as these situations appear, they all have the same solution in common: communication. If you and your partner are on different pages in terms of sexual activity, talk about it. You just might be able to reach some sort of compromise. If changes in your body cause pain with intercourse—or if you're concerned about sexually transmitted diseases—talk to your gynecologist.

This stage of life requires a high level of conversation for those difficult subjects. Whether you believe it or not, everything is negotiable. Perhaps you have a history of not seeing eye-to-eye or avoiding confrontations, but what do you have to lose by speaking your mind and your truth? That's a question that deserves some deep thought and introspection. Because if you can't stand up for yourself and your own needs, who is going to do it for you?

At the age of seventy-five, Gina claims that she'll be working on her emotional wounds until the day she dies. Those wounds include growing up with alcoholic parents, getting a divorce at sixty-two, moving a thousand miles away from her ex-husband, going back to work at sixty-five, and dealing with a gambling addiction. She didn't complain about her ex (although she certainly had good cause), but instead sought out professional advice, figured out what she needed and wanted, created a plan, and took appropriate action. She took care of herself and did it all without drama and has no regrets. Was it easy? No. Was it necessary? Yes.

Gina certainly isn't the only person to leave a long-term marriage. What follows is a somewhat complicated and unlikely tale involving the end of two long-term marriages and the beginning of a love story that has defied all odds and demonstrates just how complicated relationships can be.

When Lesley and Keri were twelve, they met on the bus during a five-hour ride to summer camp. They became fast friends, shared a bunk bed every summer for the next four years, and spent countless hours on the phone when they weren't together.

When they turned sixteen, Keri developed an interest in boys and pulled away from the friendship. Lesley was heartbroken. Over time, she developed a partnership with another woman, Keri got married to a man, and the two drifted apart.

Lesley had been married to her partner for twenty-five years when she again heard from Keri, who found her on the internet. A reunion ensued, and the friends were overjoyed to reconnect. Lesley realized she was still very attracted to Keri, but out of respect for both of their marriages, she said nothing.

Three months later, Keri was diagnosed with stage IV lung cancer and was given a prognosis of eighteen months. She confided in Lesley that her marriage had been dead for years, and what she really wanted before she died was romance and love. Lesley had also been in a rocky marriage and longed for kindness and peace. In spite of their admissions, the two women returned to their respective relationships.

For the next two years, Keri underwent chemotherapy, radiation, brain surgery, and the removal of a lung. She and Lesley communicated via texts and emails and allowed themselves to fall in love. In time, Keri filed for divorce. Lesley followed suit, and moved 3,000 miles to be close to Keri and start a new life.

Lesley and Keri married in October 2015, five years after Keri's diagnosis. Today, Keri is in remission and maintains regular visits with her oncologist. The two women do whatever they can to make the most out of every day they share.

MAKING AMENDS

Before we end our discussion of relationships, let's talk about unresolved issues with adult children, other family members, and friends. Sometimes—in the case of addiction or serious moral infractions—you must cut the cord. Other times, it's important to make amends or consider being the person who makes things right. You're the only one who knows the correct course of action, but if a situation has been gnawing at you, you might want to take time to reconsider a previous decision.

Sometimes a relationship is so toxic and unhealthy that walking away is the only option. Other times, the feud becomes trivial and continues to exist only because no one is big enough to apologize. What about that friendship that ended over something so small you can't even remember the circumstances?

There is some truth to the adage "time heals all wounds." If you are compelled to attempt to make peace, we encourage you to do it. That doesn't mean your advances will be accepted, but being the bigger person and taking the high road is always recommended as long as you're sincere in your efforts.

If you're not sure about what to do, imagine being at the end of your life. Do you have any regrets about the way you handled a particular relationship? If you do, consider making a phone call, sending an email, or writing a letter. If you're fine with the way things turned out and you're glad that the raving lunatic/competitive bitch/opinionated critic is out of your life, then let it go.

Wendy Satsky

Wendy and Marc met at a mutual friend's birthday party in New Jersey when they were fifteen and a half—still so young that they measured their ages in half-year increments. They shared a kiss that night, but shortly afterward Marc left for boarding school in upstate New York.

Their first real date occurred six weeks later when Marc returned home over school break and invited Wendy to a surprise outing in New York. They took the bus into the city on a beautiful October evening, and their first stop was a restaurant owned by Marc's aunt and uncle. Instead of staying for dinner, however, Marc picked up an envelope from his aunt and proceeded to take Wendy to a Chinese restaurant.

"We sat on the upper level and had nonalcoholic drinks with little umbrellas in them," she recalls. "It was all so festive and grown-up! After dinner, we walked to the Winter Garden Theatre on Broadway and it was there that my surprise was revealed. The envelope Marc received from his aunt contained two tickets to 'Funny Girl' with Barbra Streisand. It was the most perfect first date imaginable!"

Marc returned to school a few days later, and the fledgling couple tried to maintain a long-distance relationship. Four months later, on Valentine's Day, Marc sent Wendy a Candygram—then broke up with her by phone later that day.

"He started talking about how hard it was to keep a relationship going when we were so far apart, and then he just dumped me. I was devastated, and I remember sitting on the sofa in my parents' living room, listening to Beatles' songs and crying my eyes out."

For the next few years, the two saw each other whenever Marc was home from school, but they made no attempt to rekindle their romance. After graduating from prep school, Marc headed to the University of Denver and Wendy attended a local college in New Jersey. They stayed in touch—still just as friends—and Wendy decided to make a trip to Colorado to see him after graduation.

"I'd never been west of Pennsylvania in my life," she explains, "and I wanted to do something fun and adventurous before officially entering the work force in the fall."

What was intended to be a one-week visit turned into a month. Wendy fell in love with Colorado, and the spark that had always existed with Marc seemed to flare during her stay. But still they didn't act on it. She returned to New Jersey and began to prepare for her teaching job, while he forged a real estate career in Denver.

On Labor Day weekend in 1969, shortly after returning from Colorado, Wendy rekindled a relationship with Stuart—a classic "bad boy" whom she had dated briefly the previous summer. His tough, edgy persona was the direct result of a difficult early life. Born in a home for unwed mothers in Nova Scotia, he was adopted by a couple from New Jersey when he was eighteen months old. His father died when Stuart was twelve, and he became the sole caretaker for his mother, who was ill for most of her life.

Although he was in the habit of shielding his thoughts and feelings from others, Stuart opened up to Wendy. He made her feel special and important, and she fed on the attention he heaped upon her.

"Looking back, I can see that I had a very immature concept of relationships," she tells us. "Stuart was very jealous and insecure, and that made him cling to me. In the beginning I was flattered and perceived it as incredibly deep love, and that was precisely what I needed at the time. Our early years were exciting, fun, and rebellious—a true reflection of the early seventies."

In 1971, Wendy and Stuart went on a hitchhiking adventure to New Mexico, Colorado, and California. It was on this trip that Stuart became enamored with Colorado, sharing Wendy's love for the area. They fantasized about living there one day, although it seemed like nothing more than a dream at the time.

In May of 1973, when Wendy was twenty-six and Stuart was twenty-eight, they married and moved into an apartment in New Jersey. A year later, while Marc was visiting his parents, he stopped by and met Stuart for the first time. The two men got along well and eventually became good friends.

For the next few years, Stuart worked as a real estate appraiser. Wendy gave birth to their daughter, Danielle, on Christmas Day in 1974. They still dreamed of moving to Colorado, and that dream suddenly took shape in the fall of 1978.

Stuart's sister and her husband had been living in Colorado, where they'd bought a local trash company. One day, out of the blue, she called and offered Stuart a job driving a trash truck. He couldn't say yes fast enough.

When Stuart, Wendy, and Danielle arrived in Vail, the aspens were in full glory. Stuart started his job in waste management, then left a year later to return to his career as an appraiser. Wendy was teaching, Danielle was thriving, and all seemed right in their world. In 1983, Wendy gave birth to Ben.

Because they weren't far from Denver, where Marc lived, they saw him on a regular basis. They stayed at his house whenever they were in the city, and he frequently joined them in Vail to ski. Marc was often in a relationship—a few of them long term—but he had never married.

"Marc was a big part of our family in those days," says Wendy. He was like a godfather to Danielle and Ben, and they called him Uncle Markie."

Fast forward twenty years, when a news story broke about the illegally operated maternity home where Stuart spent his early life. He attended a reunion of the others who lived there, and the sordid story of his past—including the deaths of many babies—was revealed.

Stuart returned home from the reunion deeply scarred. Racked with survivor's guilt, he fell into a severe depression. His health began to decline, but no one thought his problems were anything but emotional.

In the fall of 2004, six years after the reunion, Stuart was diagnosed with advanced-stage adrenal cortical cancer. It's likely, his doctor said, that he had been sick for at least six years.

Stuart's diagnosis caused him to turn inward even more. He became paranoid and easily threatened, distancing himself from all his friends. Marc often called to try to reconnect, but Stuart would either respond rudely or simply hang up. This behavior continued until the following January, when Stuart finally agreed to let Marc and a few other friends visit him.

"There seemed to be some forgiveness going on," Wendy recalls. "Stuart had been so cruel to them, particularly Marc, and I could sense that there was regret."

Two months after making amends, Stuart passed away.

Following Stuart's death, Marc would call Wendy once a week to see how she was doing. She was grateful for his friendship, and she would occasionally travel to Denver to meet him for lunch or dinner.

In June of 2006, widowed for more than a year, Wendy attended a concert in Denver with Marc. They ended up spending the weekend together, then started seeing each other more frequently.

"It didn't become a 'thing' until some time in 2007," she remembers. "It was easy to be with Marc...we were so spontaneous...and I enjoyed that. My marriage to Stuart required a lot of mental energy, and I often felt like I had to walk on eggshells. He was very wary of others, and I made sure to think through anything he might perceive as a threat."

Although Wendy was happy with Marc, her grown children were not quick to embrace the relationship. While not overtly opposed to it, they seemed to express their displeasure passively: ignoring Marc on occasion and not demonstrating much interest in Wendy and Marc's life together.

Torn between her love for Marc and her love for her children, Wendy decided to see a therapist. In those sessions, she learned a very important lesson: she didn't need to apologize to anyone for her feelings.

Wendy wrote her daughter a letter, gently explaining that her marriage to Stuart had not always been an easy one. She shared that she was happy with Marc, and although she didn't expect Danielle to approve, she hoped they could find common ground and learn to respect their differences.

"Not having my daughter's support was painful," says Wendy, "and I did a lot of soul-searching before writing to her. It's been a challenge, to be sure. In those difficult moments when I could see that both Danielle and Ben were suffering from the loss of their dad, I knew I had to find a way to be sensitive to their feelings while being true to my own."

Two years ago—shortly after Ben's first child was born—Danielle, her husband, and their two daughters visited Colorado. They spent a few days in the mountains with Ben, his wife, and the new baby, then drove to Denver to see Wendy and Marc. After they finished dinner and the girls were put to bed, the four stayed up and talked nearly all night. Danielle and her husband said they wanted to move from their home in Oregon to Colorado, and Wendy was thrilled that her family would all be living in the same state.

"It felt so normal and comfortable," Wendy recalls with a big smile. It's as if the baby brought us all together."

Today, the entire clan lives in Colorado. They frequently spend time together, and Wendy loves being near her children and grandchildren. She and Marc recently bought a home together and are planning to marry.

"It's been a difficult road for all of us," she says. "It's hard when your perceptions are so different than those of your children, but I think it's important to acknowledge your feelings. It wasn't easy to stand my ground when faced with resistance, but I realized that I had every right to follow my heart.

"As time goes by, Marc and I are getting better at keeping our hearts open. I'm very grateful to have him as my partner—a man with awareness, sensitivity, patience, and a willingness to communicate. He has brought an enormous amount of joy into my life—although I don't think I'll ever forgive him for dumping me on Valentine's Day."

SPENDING TIME ALONE

Although relationships are a key ingredient to a happy life, it's also important to have enough alone time to collect your thoughts, plan your days, and contemplate life. Some women hate the prospect of being alone, so they plan every minute of the day, making sure their social calendars are teeming with an array of activities or busywork.

In truth, the result of such a flurry is quantity, but not necessarily quality. If this sounds familiar, we suggest that you set aside a day to think about your life and take stock of the people who are in it. If you truly enjoy your frenetic schedule, by all means continue doing what works. But if your activities are merely a Band-Aid for a deeply rooted fear of being alone or a means to sidestep grief, you might want to delve into the situation and see if there's a way to create more balance. We need people, but we also need to be comfortable... alone...in our own skin.

ACTION STEPS

I am willing to foster relationships—both existing and new—by taking the following action. (Check all that apply.)	
I will look online for meet-ups, community college classes, and clubs in my area.	
I will join at least one group and regularly attend meetings.	
I will begin conversations by asking open-ended questions about people I meet.	
I will reach out to my friends and family and schedule a coffee or lunch date.	
When I feel lonely, I will pick up the phone and call a friend.	
I will make sure I factor in time to be alone to contemplate life or simply read a good book.	

Chapter 5

Ain't Misbehavin'—or Are You?

"When you're the victim of the behavior, it's black and white;
when you're the perpetrator, there are a million shades of gray."
*—*Laura Schlessinger, American talk radio host

So...that thing you do...that attitude you project...over and over and over...how's it working for you?

To be sure, we are all creatures of habit. In many cases, our behaviors were shaped in early childhood and integrated so seamlessly into our adult lives that we don't recognize them as self-sabotaging or downright destructive. In fact, we don't even acknowledge them at all. They are simply an element of who we are—as much a part of our DNA as blue eyes or olive skin. Or so we think.

We have Facebook pages with hundreds of followers, yet when we posted a request for women to share their bad habits, only one replied. One! To us, that's absolute proof of the fact that most people aren't even remotely aware of the things they do that get in the way.

Well, we just can't let that continue, can we? It's time to acknowledge the things you do that undermine relationships, affect your emotional health and well-being, annoy the heck out of others—or worse, harm them emotionally—and compromise your peace of mind. Somewhere deep inside, you know what the issue is. You just have to be willing to stare it in the face and do something about it.

What will it be? How important is it?

I have more good habits than most people I know, and I am always trying to make better choices.									
1	2	3	4	5	6	7	8	9	10

I am willing to look honestly at my behaviors to identify and change anything that is causing pain or dysfunction in my life or the lives of others.									
1	2	3	4	5	6	7	8	9	10

If I can't change a particular behavior on my own, I get the help and support I need.									
1	2	3	4	5	6	7	8	9	10

I understand how important it is to stop repeating destructive and/or annoying patterns, and I do my best to contain them.									
1	2	3	4	5	6	7	8	9	10

I apologize when my behavior offends or harms someone.									
1	2	3	4	5	6	7	8	9	10

I accept the consequences for any and all of my actions.									
1	2	3	4	5	6	7	8	9	10

If, like Mary Poppins, you're "perfect in every way," we wish you the best in maintaining your delusions. But if you're a mere mortal like the rest of us, there's plenty of room for improvement and, at this stage of life, time to work on refining some of those habits that keep you from being as joyful and enjoyable as you could be.

If you're not sure where to begin, the following review of bad habits and their antonyms should help. We've come up with a few common examples to help you recognize and replace the traditions that no longer serve you. Even implementing one or two of them can make a huge difference in your life. People who know you well will notice that something is different and better about you, even if they might not be able to put their finger on it. It's kind of like the perfect facelift: effective, yet not glaringly obvious.

Habit: Controlling. You're not very willing to compromise, and it seems that the older you get, the more unyielding you become. You like things to be a certain way, and when that doesn't happen—when something changes—you're not happy.

You get pissy if someone in spin class takes your favorite bike. You're always the one who brings biscotti to your weekly bridge game, and you go quiet for an entire hour when the new girl brings a treat that flaunts her baking skills. When you show up for your first day of volunteering at the animal shelter, you immediately start revising their procedures because your way is the best—and only—way.

Solution: Flexible. It's perfectly acceptable to want to control your own life, but you don't get to universally impose your wants and wishes on others. Digging in your heels and insisting upon having things just the way you like them serves no purpose other than to alienate those around you. Learn to distinguish between suggestions and commands. Step back and think before you overreact.

Will it really compromise your workout if you're on the spin bike by the windows instead of the one in front of the instructor? Is there a possibility that the new girl's cupcakes are delicious and she'll share her recipe with you? Does it matter to the pound puppies if they get treats before or after their walks?

If you don't consider alternatives...if you don't give others a chance to rise to the occasion...you're imposing limits that are less than helpful for all concerned. You also run the risk of coming across as a rigid old bitch, and no one wants that. Life will be a lot more fun—and probably a lot more satisfying—when you let go.

Habit: Insensitive. You're fairly detached from the plights of others. You can't be bothered with the issues your friends are facing, and as long as their problems don't affect you directly, you're cool with it. People may accuse you of being cold and uncaring, but too bad. You have your own stuff to worry about.

Your best friend calls to say she's miserably lonely and would love to find a nice guy. You suggest she try online dating, and then make an excuse to get off the phone. You have zero tolerance for any type of behavior that you deem rude, whether it's the speeding driver weaving in and out of traffic or the elderly woman in front of you in the check-out line who's holding up the works with her handbag full of coupons. Every Mother's Day, you wait for the-call-that-never-comes from your adopted daughter who lives in another state. It doesn't matter that this has been the case since she moved out—you still get angry when the day comes and goes without a word from her.

Solution: Compassionate. For many of us, being compassionate is not a place we go easily. Getting there requires some work, but it can be done. When someone frustrates you, irritates you, or merely bores the hell out of you with their chronic complaints, take a deep breath and pause before you respond. It's better to say or do nothing than react in a way that you'll later regret.

Offer to help your friend fill out her online dating profile, then peruse photos of available men and laugh at the ones who are wearing tank tops. Give the speeding driver a break, because he might be rushing his asthmatic child to the ER. Stop looking at your watch and be patient with the woman in the grocery store. Perhaps she's living on a fixed income, and those coupons make all the difference between eating a nutritious meal and not eating at all. Look beyond your own needs on Mother's Day and try to see it from your daughter's perspective. Maybe the day is a reminder that the woman who gave birth to her abandoned her, and acknowledging it in any way is more than her emotions can handle.

You can't possibly know what motivates another's behavior, but you certainly can learn to give the benefit of the doubt and stop being unconcerned, self-righteous, or thoughtless.

Donna hated talking to her ex. Even though their three children were grown and there wasn't much cause for communication, he seemed to find excuses to call her. Each time he did, his tone was snarky and rude. He never tired of criticizing her alleged lack of good parenting skills—even though her active parenting days were long gone. She would inevitably get caught up in his negativity, responding in ways that were either angry and defensive or clipped and cold. It was a cycle they repeated over and over.

One day, recognizing his number on her cell phone, Donna impulsively decided to take a different approach. Instead of engaging in their usual destructive dialogue, she would be nice to him.

She answered with a cheery "Hi, Drew! How are you?" She then proceeded to steer the conversation onto neutral turf, asking him if he was enjoying retirement and inquiring about his progress with the small vineyard he was installing. She never gave him the opportunity to launch his usual attack and, caught completely off guard, he didn't even try. Instead, he asked her about her volunteer work and her recent trip to Spain. They talked about the kids and mused about future grandchildren. The upshot was that they had the first civilized conversation they'd had in years. With one simple shift from coldness to kindness, Donna broke a bad habit that had been destined to plague her for as long as her ex had access to a phone.

Habit: Fearful. You play worst-case-scenario at every opportunity. You're afraid you're going to get seriously ill, putting a permanent end to the fit-and-healthy lifestyle you've always enjoyed. You're going to outlive your IRA and have to subsist on ramen and peanut butter sandwiches. You're going to be alone when you're old, clad in an oatmeal-stained bathrobe and surrounded by cats.

For many women, getting older goes hand in hand with becoming more fearful. You realize that more of your life is behind you than in front of you, and the thought of running out of time creeps into your consciousness. For nearly every situation that confronts you, you can play out a negative outcome in your head. It's called overthinking, and the risk is that it can turn into a paralyzing fear.

Solution: Brave. Sooner or later, you'll have to face one or more of your fears. Whether it's declining health, lack of money, loneliness, or loss of independence, there's something out there that's nothing short of terrifying. How you choose to cope if those fears become realities will make all the difference.

If you're afraid you won't have enough money when you're older, take charge of that now. If you're retired and there's no additional income in sight, make sure you spend what you have wisely. Even if you feel flush today, there's no reason to keep buying like there's no tomorrow. There *is* a tomorrow, and you want to be able to enjoy it fully.

If your biggest fear is being old and alone, you're like many women we've interviewed. Perhaps the fact that women are social, nurturing creatures is the reason why isolation seems so frightening.

While having a significant other and/or grown kids can be a hedge against loneliness, it's not a guarantee. You could outlive your partner, so there goes that plan. As for kids, our research shows that women who have no children are afraid there won't be anyone to take care of them if they get old and infirm, yet women with children worry about being a burden. So kids or no kids, that's less than an ideal solution.

The behavior that works is cultivating friendships that you can count on for better or for worse. Alone today will likely mean alone tomorrow, so if you're relatively solitary now, this is the time to do something about it. Reach out and bring people into your life. Smile more. Embrace an attitude that lets others know you're open and welcoming.

Some things that cause fear, like unexpected illness, are beyond your control. The best you can do is to dig deep, tap into your inner warrior, and face the challenge. Please don't think you have to do this alone. Ask questions, seek help, and do the best you can, but above all else, be strong.

Courage allows us to face our fears with dignity instead of kicking and screaming when we really have no choice. When bravery is called for, it's important to keep in mind that women throughout history—from Cleopatra to Rosa Parks—have had to fight to overcome obstacles and face their fears. As Eleanor Roosevelt suggested, "Do one thing every day that scares you."

Habit: Egocentric. You're convinced that you're better—in some way or many ways—than all of your friends and acquaintances. You hold yourself on a lofty plane and stand in judgment from on high. You're smarter, classier, better dressed, better read, more sophisticated, and more talented than the average folks you see scuttling around beneath you. You work harder, exercise more intensely, eat better, and have no vices. Everything you do, everyone in your immediate family, and everything that surrounds you is utterly, magnificently fabulous.

Okay, we're exaggerating for effect, but we think you know what we mean. Some women—and we're not pointing fingers—just like to show off. If this sounds familiar, it might be time for a come-to-Jesus moment.

We'll give you the benefit of the doubt, because maybe you really have been incredibly privileged throughout your life. You've been blessed with beauty, intelligence, opportunity, and good fortune. Lucky you! But guess what? We don't want to hear about it.

No one likes a braggart. No one is impressed by someone who flaunts her greatness every chance she gets. Such behavior will not draw others to you. In fact, their reaction will likely be just the opposite. See all those people running down the road kicking up a cloud of dust as they race to get away? They used to be your friends.

Solution: Humble and Interested. If your cheeks are burning right about now, it's time to rethink your motives. Telling anyone within earshot how fabulous you are—even if you're doing it in a subtle way (if that's even possible)—is less likely to generate awe and more likely to cause people to avoid you. So instead of announcing to your barre class that you studied at the David Howard School of Ballet in New York, comment on how much your quads and glutes are burning. Instead of describing in superlatives your recent cruise to the Bahamas, ask your friend if she enjoyed the movie you just saw together. Instead of trying to upstage your dinner hostess by telling her that your lasagna was once featured in a cooking magazine—when she's serving lasagna—mention what a treat it is to enjoy good food with good friends.

Learn to listen and comment on what others have to say without making it all about you. Open up your head and heart and let people in. You just might be amazed at the warmth you feel when you genuinely connect with others.

Lisa had a habit of being mildly boastful. Her friends would occasionally roll their eyes when she'd carry on about something "unbelievably fabulous," but they just chalked it up to Lisa being Lisa and let it slide.

Suddenly, without notice, her boastfulness escalated dramatically. She began to hold court about the places she visited, the restaurants she dined in, and the designer clothes she bought. She bragged about her high-achieving kids and unparalleled cooking skills. If anyone had recently read a good book, she had read a better book. If anyone had successfully held a plank at the gym for two minutes, she'd held one for five. (We don't believe you, Lisa.) It was essential for her to outperform, outpace, and outclass anyone and everyone. All. The. Time. Her friends were getting increasingly fed up with her endless superlatives, so Sylvie, her closest buddy, volunteered to have a talk with her.

Lisa responded to Sylvie's concern with complete candidness. She confessed that her husband had been having an affair with a younger woman, and she was devastated by the discovery. She felt old, fat, ugly, and washed up. She felt insignificant and invisible, and trying to appear vital and important was her way of dealing with her insecurity. She didn't want her friends to know, because she was sure their sympathy would push her right over the emotional edge.

Sylvie helped Lisa understand that the people who loved her would continue to do so despite her cheating spouse. She didn't need to be the best at everything—she just needed to be her open and honest self.

Although her ego was suffering, Lisa tried very hard to change her ways. She learned to embrace the concern of her friends. Over time, she accepted the inevitably of a divorce and hired "the absolute world's best, most amazing, and ruthless" attorney. (Welcome back, Lisa.)

Habit: Avoiding. Your favorite movie line is the one made famous by Scarlett O'Hara: "I can't think about that right now. If I do, I'll go crazy. I'll think about that tomorrow."[18] You'll move heaven and earth in an attempt to avoid anything that you find unpleasant or difficult to face. Telling a friend that it really pisses you off when she constantly cancels plans at the last minute? Tomorrow. Booking an appointment with the dermatologist about that weird spot on your shoulder? Tomorrow. Facing up to the fact that the criticism regularly heaped on you by your spouse is, in fact, verbal abuse? Tomorrow. No matter how important it is, if it requires an emotional investment, you're outta there.

Solution: Confronting. If you're the woman with her head in the sand, it's time to look up and face the hard stuff. It's far better to acknowledge an issue—even if you're trembling when you do so—than to let it spiral out of control.

You know that ignoring a problem doesn't make it disappear, right? (Ah, but it feels oh-so-good when you pretend that the world is utterly rosy!) So take a deep breath, try to steady your voice, and tell your gee-I-can't-make-it friend that when you set aside time for the two of you to be together, it hurts your feelings when she bails time and again. You don't have to get angry or even particularly confrontational; you just have to tell her how you honestly feel. If she understands and apologizes, problem solved. If she gets belligerent and defensive, it might be time to move on. Either way, the issue disappears.

Call your dermatologist and find out if that spot really is the skin cancer you're afraid it is. Pretending it isn't there won't make it go away, and knowing exactly what you're dealing with will help you determine a course of treatment. Perhaps it's nothing serious at all. Wouldn't the relief feel better than the worrying?

Get into counseling with or without your insulting spouse. Just because he doesn't hit you doesn't mean he's not being abusive when he belittles you every chance he gets. A good therapist can be your best ally in cases like this.

Whatever you're avoiding, we promise you that coping is the first step toward a solution. Things may not turn out perfectly, but addressing and solving any issue will serve you far better than running away from it.

Habit: Critical. You're a pro at finding something wrong with just about everything, even if it has absolutely no impact on you or any part of your life. You're highly opinionated, and you're quick to verbalize your observations.

Your sister-in-law's hair is too long and too brassy. Your nephew's political beliefs are steeped in ignorance. Your neighbor really should have that unsightly mole removed. The redhead you always see at the gym should stop wearing pink. You think it, you share it—and you're not picky about whom you tell. As far as you're concerned, anyone within earshot will do.

Solution: Accepting. If this behavior rings true for you, think about it for a minute. Is the criticism really necessary? Does it serve any purpose? Does it cause anything to change?

Will your sister-in-law race to the hair salon, your nephew become a liberal, your neighbor book an appointment with a cosmetic surgeon, the redhead ask you to take her clothes shopping? Doubtful. Strike that. Impossible.

These scenarios are none of your concern and out of your control. Why waste energy on what someone else is doing, wearing, or supporting? Unless you're the direct recipient of someone else's bad habits, your opinions and observations aren't relevant.

Instead of voicing your criticism, learn to accept that there will always be people who don't reflect your beliefs and priorities. And that's okay. They're absolutely entitled to dress as they please, embrace causes they believe it, and follow whatever path makes them happy.

"Omigod! Her pants are so tight they show *everything!*"

"Those shorts are *waaaay* too short for someone her age."

"Horizontal stripes on *that* butt?"

"A hippie skirt, socks, and Birkenstocks—is she *serious?*"

"A romper on a fifty-plus woman? You've *gotta* be kidding me!"

This was Louisa's running dialogue as she walked through the mall with her friend Heidi. The two were regular shopping partners, and the mall was the perfect place for Louisa to find women whose style she deemed inferior. Today, on this sunny Saturday afternoon in early fall, Heidi had had enough.

"Do you hear yourself?" she asked Louisa, stopping dead in her tracks in front of Williams-Sonoma. "You've been criticizing people nonstop for the past twenty minutes, and I've just about had it!"

Louisa was so shocked by Heidi's words that her eyes filled with tears. The two women had never had as much as a minor spat, so this sudden outburst shook her to the core. Her emotions ran from embarrassed to hurt and back again, and she was—for the first time in a long time—at a complete loss for words.

"I love you, LouLou, but this has got to stop," Heidi continued. "You're so judgmental of everything, and it's starting to wear on me. If you're not making fun of how people dress, you're complaining about the morons at work. Or how tacky your son's girlfriend is. You nitpick everything and everyone! Why on earth would you choose to fill your life with such negativity?"

The utter intensity of Heidi's outburst was the wake-up call that Louisa needed. She apologized humbly and vowed on the spot to think before speaking. She truly had not been aware of her pattern of criticism, and the realization shamed and devastated her. At that very moment, changing her ways became the most important task of her life.

Habit: Hopeless. You're convinced you're never going to lose fifteen pounds before your class reunion, so you console yourself with a cheeseburger and fries. You drop the Italian class you were taking in preparation for your trip to Florence because you failed the first two tests and are obviously too stupid to learn a new language. Your boyfriend walked out, your daughter moved three states away, and your best friend is spending most of her time with a woman she met at the farmers' market. You're feeling utterly forsaken and abandoned.

Solution: Optimistic. We promise not to insult you with platitudes like "Chin up!" "Look on the bright side!" "Tomorrow will be a better day!" We can already hear you muttering "bullshit," and that's not where we want to go with you. Instead, we'd like to point out a few things that might alter your perspective.

Re: the class reunion...do you really think anyone is going to look anything like they did forty or fifty years ago? Over time, tummies bulge, butts flatten, and upper arms sway in the breeze. Faces wrinkle, hair grays and thins, and brown spots appear everywhere. Why should you be any different? So screw the fifteen pounds because they simply don't matter. (Although we'd like to mention that the burger and fries are pure sabotage, so you might want to rethink that.) Cut yourself some slack, find a nice dress in your closet (even buy a new one if you must), and go meet your former high-school buddies with a spring in your step and a smile on your face.

Re: the failed tests...do you honestly believe you're stupid? Are you "slow of mind, given to unintelligent decisions or acts, or lacking intelligence or reason?" Because that's how Merriam-Webster defines "stupid," and performing poorly on a couple of Italian tests hardly qualifies. Instead of labeling yourself and giving in to defeat, listen to some language tapes and give it another shot. No matter how far you take it, you'll emerge knowing more Italian than you do now. And with a phrase book in your pocket and a willingness to communicate in your heart, you'll do fine. (It's also important to note that, in our experience, Italians are so polite that they'll tell you your accent is *eccellente* even if you greet them with an ear-jarring "*Bon joorno.*")

Re: feeling forsaken...is there a possibility you might be overgeneralizing? Are the three people who are no longer a big part of your life the only people in your circle? Look around. Odds are there are others whose presence gives you hope. Expand your mental horizons and be open to the possibilities. If you've truly been sheltered and there's no one to play with, we suggest you re-read the chapter on relationships for ideas on how to make new friends.

Habit: Apathetic. Your neighbor just told you that a member of the local city council has been brought up on corruption charges. *Yawn.* There's a new cocktail lounge in town that's drawing folks older than twenty-five. *Yawn.* Your girlfriends are going to the coast for a spa weekend. *Yawn.*

Whether it's the latest political news, a fun hot spot to try, or socializing with your best buds, these days you're not interested in much of anything. You often feel that you can't possibly keep up with the pace of life today, so you slow down. Apathy sets in. The hours creep by ever so slowly. You're bored out of your mind, and it has become a pattern.

Solution: Goal-driven. It is important to remember that lack of interest and lack of motivation are not issues that are happening to you. They are, in fact, created by you. If you think your life is blah, it will be blah. And once you enter the spiral of negative thoughts, the ride down can be a long and unpleasant one.

The good news is that you can do something about it. Start by creating value-driven goals that will give you something specific to focus on and pursue. The first thing, which is painfully obvious, is to figure out what you want, and the best way to do that is to take a look at who you are.

Despite aging—despite changes in your appearance and your health—your fundamental essence is still the same. Are you a helper, an adventurer, an achiever, or a peacemaker? Are you happiest when you are assisting others, creating something, or engaging in a professional pursuit? Answering questions like these will put you back in touch with who you are at your core. To help you along, take a look at the Enneagram of Personality[19] or take the Myers-Briggs test[20] online.

Your goal can be large or small, meaningful or frivolous. It can be a trip to Venice, a Mercedes convertible, or the perfect little black dress you've been trying to find since you were thirty-five. It can be more money in the bank for your old age, better communication with your spouse, or a doable relationship with your sweet-but-lazy grown son who refuses to move out of the house, goddammit. It can be a part-time job, reconciliation with your estranged sibling, or converting the spare bedroom into a walk-in closet.

The point is that it's *your* goal, so it doesn't matter if someone else might criticize it or make fun of it. It simply has to have value to you.

Ever since Sally saw the movie "Born Free" when she was sixteen, she's wanted to visit Kenya. Throughout her lifetime, something always stood in the way of getting there: the requisite summer jobs during college, launching a career, paying rent, getting married, raising children, maintaining a home. Looking back, she admits that some of those reasons were merely excuses. Although she was excited and intrigued by the idea of such an adventure, she was also nervous and intimidated.

Fast forward to present day, which finds Sally age sixty-eight, widowed, retired from her work as an accountant, and frequent babysitter to her twin grandchildren. Although she loves the little ones, caring for them isn't how she expected to spend this phase of her life.

"I felt so lost with no career and no husband, and I didn't know what to do. So every time my daughter asked me to babysit, I said yes. I managed to settle into a routine, and I was bored and miserable. I knew I needed something more, and then it hit me. I still wanted to visit Kenya, and I realized it wasn't too late. Sorry, kiddies, but grandma has places to go!"

So Sally started a freelance bookkeeping business. She created a website, placed an ad in the local paper, posted notices on the co-op and church bulletin boards, and told everyone she knew. As word spread, she managed to secure one local client and added three more over six months. Within a year, she had a profitable dozen and a ticket to Nairobi.

"Finally!" she exudes. "I'm still a little nervous, but this time I'm not going to let fear get in my way. After waiting this long, I'm going to make sure this is the trip of a lifetime!"

Habit: Comparing Yourself to Others. You are incapable of entering a room without looking around to see how you stack up compared to other women. Depending on what you see/assess, you either hold your head high or slink into a corner. God forbid you should show up for a new class at the gym, only to find a room full of twenty-somethings with butts higher than your cholesterol and skin that's still firmly attached to their bodies. Perish the thought of going to a cocktail party and discovering that all the women are wearing black—and you're decked out in bright red.

Social media makes your comparison habit even worse. A simple scroll through your Facebook feed reveals your friends' exotic vacations, cooking prowess, perfect relationships, and accomplished offspring. Based on how they appear to be living their lives, you and your family look like a bunch of slugs.

Solution: Being Comfortable with Who You Are. We hate to break it to you, girlfriend, but just about everywhere you go, you will see someone who is prettier, younger, taller, thinner, curvier, or fitter. Someone who is smarter, funnier, sassier, classier, richer, or braver. Someone who is more charming, more talented, more quick-witted, more sophisticated, more interesting, or more elegant. And to that we say: so fucking what?

Eleanor Roosevelt addressed the issue best—and she didn't even need to drop the F bomb—when she said, "No one can make you feel inferior without your consent." Think about it for a minute. The comparison is coming from within you, not from someone else. Do you really believe that the statuesque woman waiting in line for a drink during theatre intermission is looking at you and thinking, *Gee, she's short.* Is there a possibility that the young girls at BodyPump are impressed that a woman of your age puts a premium on strength and fitness? Can it be that at least one of the women in black at the cocktail party is wishing she'd had the nerve to wear a bold color?

You are who you are, and being comfortable with whatever that looks like is one of the keys to your happiness. You've been around for quite a while, so it's time to accept your imperfections, honor your strong points, and embrace the combination of the two.

Habit: Collecting/Hoarding. Every surface in your home is covered with some sort of tchotchke: the collection of frogs your mother started for you when you were six, marble coasters from all the wineries you visited in the Napa Valley on your tenth wedding anniversary, Mason jars filled with beach glass. Your kitchen cupboard is overflowing with a random assortment of mugs commemorating Mother's Day and your birthday, touting World's Best Mom and #1 Scrabble Player, advertising places you don't remember visiting, and attesting to the benefits of caffeine. You've kept prom dresses, bridesmaid dresses, and every formal gown you've ever worn. You have boxes of costume jewelry that you inherited from your great-aunt, none of which reflect your style or taste. You've stashed away every piece of art your kids created between pre-school and eighth grade, but you're not quite sure where it is. The bottom line: if it ever had meaning, you've kept it.

Solution: De-Cluttering. Wouldn't it be nice to have a side table in your home with room to plunk down the book you've been reading? How nice would it be to free up closet space for the clothes you actually wear? Can you imagine the convenience of opening a kitchen cupboard and being able to see exactly what's inside?

Whether you call it downsizing, reducing clutter, or finally dealing with all the items you've amassed over the years, it's an issue that really should be addressed. It will only get worse as time goes by, so now is the time to take action and streamline your space. If you need help sorting and tossing (or if you're embarrassed by years of haphazardly accumulating treasures), hire a professional home organizer to help. If this concept is new to you, you can learn more about it on Angie's List.[21]

Keep in mind that collecting is very different from hoarding, which usually involves saving random items and storing them haphazardly. Hoarding is a compulsive psychiatric disorder, so we'll leave it to the mental-health professionals.

Kweethai Neill, PhD

Dr. Kweethai Neill, known professionally as Dr. Kweethai, taught health at the university level and served as a department chair before becoming a clinical hypno-therapist. She is the founder and president of iHealth Center for Integrated Wellness in Roanoke, Texas, where she employs both Eastern traditions and Western scientific training. She is the author of Hypnotherapy: An Alternative Path to Health and Happiness. She offers insight on how hypnotherapy can help people make the necessary changes to lead healthier and happier lives.

"Close your eyes," Dr. Kweethai directs. "Relax and take a deep breath. Now...don't think about elephants. Whatever you do, don't think about elephants, especially those big floppy ears. No elephants, understand?"

And so begins the interview with Dr. Kweethai.

AUTHORS: *Of course it's impossible to think of anything but elephants! What just happened here?*

DR. KWEETHAI: Cognitively, you understand that you're not supposed to think about elephants. However, your subconscious mind does not discrimi-nate, so my qualifying words "do not" have no meaning. You cannot think about something negative—in this case, elephants—without unintentionally rein-forcing it in the subconscious. You hear the word "elephant" and the whole herd shows up. In essence, your subconscious mind programs your behavior. That's why hypnosis is all about.

AUTHORS: *Can you explain more about that?*

DR. KWEETHAI: Hypnosis is a natural state of consciousness—commonly called "trance"—in which your awareness is heightened while your cognition rests. In this state of mind, you are most open to suggestions made directly to your subconscious. People experience this state on a regular basis, and road trance is a perfect example. Let's take a look at that.

You're driving down the highway and a song comes on the radio that momentarily transports you back to your first school dance. You continue to drive, maintaining awareness of the traffic around you, while at the same time reminiscing about an event that occurred forty years ago. You see yourself as a teen—the clothes you wore and the style of your hair. You taste the cherry lip gloss that was your favorite in those days. You see the decorated gym and hear the shuffling of shoes on the dance floor.

What's happening is called road trance, an altered state of consciousness. Because driving can be repetitious and monotonous, being behind the wheel relaxes your cognitive mind, allowing your subconscious to take a trip into your past. You are obviously not unconscious or asleep. Rather, you remain sufficiently aware of your surroundings to continue operating a motor vehicle while simultaneously experiencing a separate reality.

There's also movie trance, book trance, and advertisement trance, all of which can transport your subconscious.

AUTHORS: *What are the applications for hypnosis?*

DR. KWEETHAI: Hypnosis is commonly used to evoke changes in personal behaviors. For example, it can be used to alter a bad habit or to help you get out of a toxic relationship. It can be used to achieve goals, such as increasing proficiency at a specific task, maximizing effectiveness in your job, or being a less reactionary parent to your adult kids. Practically anything you can put your mind to can be influenced by hypnosis.

A trained professional uses hypnosis to remove old ideas and patterns, replacing them with new suggestions. This helps people who are experiencing challenging life situations to get unstuck. One of the most exciting things about it is that people can be trained in self-hypnosis to support the changes introduced during the formal hypnotherapy sessions.

AUTHORS: *In terms of changing bad behaviors, how does hypnotherapy compare to traditional psychotherapy?*

DR. KWEETHAI: Psychotherapy often focuses on getting to the heart of why a particular behavior exists—and it can sometimes take a very long time to get there. Let's say you have a bizarre fear of brown cows. Over time, psychotherapy reveals that you were chased through a field by a brown cow when you were five. Great. Now you have the why, but you're still terrified of the beasts!

Similarly, if you've been making bad choices for fifty-five years, the why is essentially irrelevant. Knowing the reason behind your behavior doesn't make it change on the spot. Hypnotherapy, on the other hand, can stop the movie that's playing in your mind and reconfigure it, allowing you to make real and lasting change without having to wait months, or years, to do so. In fact, few therapeutic modalities are as effective as hypnotherapy in evoking behavior changes in such a short time and with no side effects.

AUTHORS: *Why do people seek out hypnotherapy?*

DR. KWEETHAI: Most people who turn to hypnotherapy are looking for a way to manage unpleasant situations or change unhealthy behaviors. Hypnotherapy helps alleviate suffering from physical pain, emotional trauma, and spiritual emptiness. It can help you lose weight, end alcohol and drug abuse, and end or modify relationships rooted in abuse or disrespect. Hypnosis has also been used in palliative care to eliminate the fear of dying.

AUTHORS: *What does it feel like to be in a hypnotic state?*

DR. KWEETHAi: When in trance, you experience extraordinary mental, physical, and emotional relaxation. This sensation is unique to hypnosis, because the quality of relaxation is different from sleep or a drug-induced state of mind. Interestingly, the term "hypnosis" comes from Hypnos, the Greek god of sleep, but it is actually a state of consciousness quite distinct from sleep.

You also experience a heightened sense of awareness during hypnotherapy. You feel that you can hear better, see more clearly, and have an increased capacity for taste, smell, and touch. You experience past events as if you were actually there—smelling the cookies baking in your mother's kitchen or seeing the vibrant colors in your grandmother's flower garden.

AUTHORS: *What happens during a hypnotherapy session?*

DR. KWEETHAI: During hypnosis, your cognitive brain takes a rest from analytical functions. That allows the subconscious to take over, accepting new information less critically. Think of it this way: the subconscious is like early computers. Because they didn't have programs to check spelling and grammar, they accepted whatever data was typed in without discrimination.

Similarly, when you are in trance, you are more open to taking in directions and instructions.

AUTHORS: *Can you be made to do something terrible—like commit a crime—or something embarrassing—like quack like a duck—as the result of hypnosis?*

DR. KWEETHAI: Absolutely not. The assumption that you can be made to commit heinous acts has been perpetrated by books and movies, and it is a complete myth. Hypnosis cannot make you do something that you consider immoral, unethical, or illegal.

Even though you are open to suggestions during a hypnotic state, you will comply only if the suggestions are consistent with your moral compass. Nothing will happen if the directions you are given conflict with your desires or beliefs, because there is still the element of will and consent. If you truly don't want to quack like a duck, you won't. By the same token, if you really don't care about improving your diet or being less critical, no degree of trance can make you change that behavior.

AUTHORS: *Can hypnotherapy create the desire to change?*

DR. KWEETHAI: Sadly, no. That desire must come from the individual. Clients sometimes tell me they wish to change, but when asked what they are willing to give up in order to experience change, they have no answer. The fact is, a cup that is full can receive no more. Therefore, you must clarify what you want to change and be clear about what you are willing to trade for it. You must be willing to give up the old to make room for the new. You must recognize what part of your life is associated with the undesirable behavior and decide if you are ready to give it up in exchange for something that will make you happier or more peaceful.

It's like the old joke: How many therapists does it take to change a light bulb? Only one, but the light bulb has to really want to be changed.

AUTHORS: *How can someone make change happen?*

DR. KWEETHAI: Hypnotherapy works via a simple, but powerful, model of change that is based on seven fundamental ideas. Subscribing to these notions places change well within your grasp.

1. Behavior is a function of a fixed idea in your unconsciousness.

2. Ideas fixed in your mind by strong emotional energies remain stuck until they are addressed.

3. These ideas are associated with the time period during which they were created—childhood, perhaps—and produce responses according to how each idea was perceived at that age.

4. Fixed ideas created in childhood pose significant problems and suffering because the related responses are not appropriate for adults.

5. Hypnotherapy takes you back in time to the original event, accessing the emotion associated with the current behavior. This is referred to as regression.

6. The hypnotherapist helps you resolve emotional scars by leading you to understand the inappropriateness of your current responses or habits.

7. The hypnotherapist helps you reframe the event and the emotion associated with it. The result is a revised perception that allows you to develop a new and appropriate response that subsequently alleviates the suffering and alters the behavior.

AUTHORS: *Are there any negative side effects of hypnosis?*

DR. KWEETHAI: No. When you come out of the trance state, you return to full awareness, feeling relaxed and refreshed.

AUTHORS: *Can anyone go into a trance or hypnotic state?*

DR. KWEETHAI: Yes. Because it is a natural state of consciousness, any healthy individual is capable of experiencing it—as naturally as you experience falling asleep or having a dream.

AUTHORS: *What do you say to people who claim they can't be hypnotized?*

DR. KWEETHAI: Trance work is not about whether or not you can be hypnotized. It's not about ability or capacity. It's about volition and desire—whether or not you want to be hypnotized. Unless you have an organic brain dysfunction or are heavily medicated, if you can carry on a wakeful conversation, you have the capacity to go into trance.

AUTHORS: *What qualities should someone look for in a hypnotherapist?*

DR. KWEETHAI: First, it's important to verify training, experience, and reputation. Once you've done that, be sure you feel at ease and have trust in the hypnotherapist. It's always a good idea to conduct an interview before engaging his or her services. As with any other professional, you need to feel comfortable with the person's style, demeanor, and ability to interact with respect and decorum.

AUTHORS: *Do you have any final thoughts for our readers regarding hypnotherapy?*

DR. KWEETHAI: Hypnotherapy is painless, and there are no drugs or pills to take. It is so simple that many people are suspicious of whether or not the process works. What can I say? I know I have changed the lives of many people through my practice of hypnotherapy, but you don't have to take my word for it. If you are really curious, find a reputable hypnotherapist and check it out for yourself. You will be amazed!

Now that you've read about behaviors and ways to change them, it's time to look inside and identify the things you'd like to address. What action will you take to accomplish your goal?

ACTION STEPS

I am willing to eliminate one or more of my bad behaviors by taking the following action. (Check all that apply.)

I will choose the behavior I want to remedy and pick a date to start changing it or eliminating it.

I will announce my intention to some of my close friends and ask them to support my efforts.

If I can't make this change on my own, I will get counseling or attend a support group.

If I'm not successful, I won't beat myself up. I'll take a break, give the situation some thought, possibly conduct some research, and try again in a week.

I will work on changing this behavior until I am successful.

I don't expect to be perfect, but I will focus on the most egregious of my bad habits.

Chapter 6

Putting Your Best Face—and Other Body Parts—Forward

"Looking good is a commitment to yourself and others. Wigs, killer heels, Pilates, even fillers—whatever works for you, honey."
—Iman, fashion model, actress, and entrepreneur

To some women, physical appearance is extremely important. If you're one of them, looking your best is as fundamental to life as eating and sleeping.

Sara wouldn't dream of going to the supermarket without dressing in something that involved a bit of time and effort. She wouldn't be caught dead in the gym without at least a swipe of concealer, blush, and lip gloss—her hair pulled back in a tidy ponytail. If a night on the town is on her agenda, she's dressed to the nines with perfectly coiffed hair and impeccable makeup.

Her weight doesn't fluctuate much, and if she sees an extra pound or two on the scale, she cuts back on carbs and does an extra set of crunches at the gym. She gets her teeth cleaned twice a year, and she's on a first-name basis with her dermatologist. She's at the hair salon so regularly that her stylist knows her favorite movies and her kids' birthdays. Sara is willing to admit that she's chasing a moving target, but she's determined to fight this aging thing with everything she's got.

To other women, fussing with appearance is a complete waste of time and energy.

Brenda is perfectly content with her graying hair and her baggy mom jeans. Makeup makes her eyes itch, so she opts for the barefaced look. She believes that shopping for groceries is a necessity, not a fashion show, so she'll go the market in whatever she happens to be wearing when she realizes she's out of eggs. She sees the gym as a place for exerting and sweating, so her husband's T-shirt and a pair of sweats is her preferred ensemble. She has three outfits that are her go-to choices for an evening out, and she describes them as "functional, presentable, and comfortable—but not particularly fashionable."

Brenda will be the first one to tell you that she could stand to lose a few pounds, but she'll also remind you that she makes the world's best raspberry cheesecake and has no intention of depriving herself of it. Ditto for meatloaf and mashed potatoes, her favorite comfort foods.

Neither of these women is wrong, over the top (okay, maybe a little), or out of her mind. Regardless of whether or not they're at the extreme ends of the appearance spectrum, each of them is being true to herself.

Odds are you fall somewhere between Sara and Brenda. Maybe looking your best matters to a certain degree, but it's not an obsession. Maybe you never really think about your appearance and just do what comes naturally. But is it natural—or is it merely a pattern you've been duplicating for years because you haven't stopped to think about it?

The important thing to remember here is that your outside self tends to be a reflection of your inside self. To get to the heart of the matter, we're going to ask you to take stock of what you see.

Put on your go-to clothes—whatever you wear when you run out to the post office or the dry cleaner. If you usually fix your hair and put on makeup for such errands, do that, too. If a floppy hat and a bare face is your norm, that's the look we want you to duplicate. Go to the mirror and take a look. What does your daily appearance say about you, and is it the message you want to send to others?

Does your hair color flatter you? Is it time to consider wearing lipstick or switching to a shade that complements your skin tone? Would a touch of blush brighten your face? Are your clothes in style, or are you still wearing remnants of the eighties and nineties? Are you in desperate need of a makeover? Resist the urge to ask a friend or partner what they think. This is about what *you* think.

My overall daily appearance suits me. I'm happy with my personal style.

1	2	3	4	5	6	7	8	9	10

I regularly replace my wardrobe with new pieces and give away or consign older pieces.

1	2	3	4	5	6	7	8	9	10

I ask my hair stylist to recommend a cut and color that work well with my hair type and flatter my face.

1	2	3	4	5	6	7	8	9	10

If I feel the need for a makeover, I'll go someplace where I can take advantage of the free services of a personal shopper (stores like Nordstrom and Bloomingdale's).

1	2	3	4	5	6	7	8	9	10

I like to wear makeup, and I'll occasionally have it done by a pro at a department store so I can stay up to speed on new products that might work well for me.

1	2	3	4	5	6	7	8	9	10

I'm okay with the way I look when I'm naked, and wearing a bathing suit at the beach or pool doesn't terrify me.

1	2	3	4	5	6	7	8	9	10

If you're happy with the way you look, hurrah! If you're not satisfied, however, we offer tips and strategies that can help you boost your appearance factor. Let's start by looking in your closet.

CLOTHING

How much of what you own do you really wear? Does the thought of purging clothes strike fear in your heart? If so, you can follow this tried-and-true exercise for weeding out your least-loved—therefore least-worn—items.

Organize your closet so all the hangers are facing backward. When you select an article of clothing to wear, replace it with the hanger turned frontward. After a year, take note of all the hangers that are still turned away from you. See those clothes? Ditch 'em. Take them to a consignment shop, offer them to a friend, sell them online, or give them to a thrift store. Just get them out of your closet, because they're taking up unnecessary space. (P.S. This rule does not pertain to special-occasion dresses or your grandmother's mink, which might rarely be worn.)

The next step is to critically evaluate what's left. You can do this on your own or engage the services of a girlfriend, which in our opinion is a lot more fun. Try things on and judge them based on style, color, and fit.

Is the style current?

Does the color flatter your skin tone?

Does the fit enhance your figure and disguise any physical flaws—real or perceived—that you may be concerned about?

If the answer is "no" to any of the above, say bye-bye and put it in the giveaway or sell pile.

Looking your best means dressing for your body type. You don't have to be long and lean to shine in clothes (but lucky you if that's what you've been blessed with). Simply knowing the type of body you have and dressing to make the most of it is all you need. Here are the basic female shapes:

Apple—Full bust, full middle

Hourglass—Full bust, small waist, full bottom

Inverted triangle—Wide shoulders, full bust, narrow hips

Pear—Small top, larger bottom

Rectangle—Shoulder, waist, and hips about the same width

Fashion model—Tall and slender

Once you've established your body type—or a combination thereof—get online to find out how to dress for it. There are masses of resources to guide you. If you're not sure how to define your shape, you can find that online, too. There are also scores of books on the best way to dress for how you're built.

What you're going to learn is that dressing appropriately for your particular body type is all about balancing your proportions. A perfect body is absolutely, positively, unequivocally not a requirement for looking stylish and fashionable.

LAYING THE PROPER FOUNDATION

We cannot stress this enough: even the most fabulous outfit will fail miserably if you're not wearing the right undergarments. According to Allied Market Research,[22] "The compression wear and shapewear market is expected to reach $5,576 million, globally by 2022." And there's a good reason for that.

The purpose of shapewear is to smooth the body's lumps and bumps so clothing drapes better and looks more streamlined. (It is not intended to make a size 14 look like a size 4.) Given advancements in fabric technology, these garments can actually be comfortable—we're not talking your mother's girdle here—as long as you don't wear them a size or two smaller than you should.

Shapewear is available in many forms—designed to chisel the midriff, waist, thighs, and butt. If you're not thrilled with any of those body parts, a trip to the lingerie department can make a world of difference. And while you're there, consider getting fitted for a bra.

According to a study conducted by myintimacy.com, the average woman's breasts will "change shape, size, and distribution at least six times during the course of her life." And we all know that one of those six times occurs after menopause. As age and gravity pull breasts downward, the key is to lift them back up to where they used to be.

Sam Saboura, a Los Angeles-based stylist who dresses a lot of celebrities, was holding a book-signing shortly after *Sam Saboura's Real Style* [23] was published. An older woman in the audience raised her hand and asked him about the best way to dress if you're large-breasted. He invited her to the front of the room, then asked if it was okay to touch her. When she said yes, Sam reached behind her, grabbed her bra straps, and pulled them upward. Instantly, her pendulous breasts lifted about three inches, making her torso look longer and giving her an overall leaner appearance. The change was so remarkably dramatic that the people in the audience literally gasped.

The message here is to never underestimate the power of a good-quality, well-fitting bra. The lingerie departments in most major retail stores feature the services of fit specialists who can offer you that same dramatic change—and comfort, to boot. It really is possible to create the appearance of the breasts you had in your youth—at least when you're clothed. If your desire is for perky breasts when you're naked, it's going to cost a bit more than a $72 bra.

HAIR

Let's get the bad news out of the way upfront: the glossy locks of youth are long gone. The aging process is no kinder to our hair than it is to any other body part, and we get hit from all sides.

Hormonal changes can cause hair to fall out—although it's a safe bet that it will miraculously show up in another unwanted place. (Chin hair, ladies?) Hair follicles also get smaller as we get older, so the hairs that grow out of them are barely visible. The upshot: most of us simply don't have as much hair as we used to, forcing us to accept the fact that thin is in.

Hair also becomes drier with age, because our oil glands aren't producing the way they used to. Elasticity becomes a thing of the past, so hair gets increasingly brittle. The lovely sleek shine that used to come naturally now has to be created with products, and while we'll never recapture that look completely, we can help it along.

From myoxin for strength to biotin for hair-loss prevention—from keratin treatments for shine to silica for building collagen—there are about as many options on the market as there are strands of hair on your head. Rather than wasting time experimenting, we suggest you consult a hair-care professional for recommendations on products or treatments that are right for you.

While you're at it, establish a relationship with that pro and aim for getting haircuts on a regular basis. A fresh cut will help maintain your style and make it easier to manage. It will also eliminate thin, frayed, and split ends, making your hair look thicker. Hair grows at a rate of about one-half inch per month, so keep that in mind when scheduling appointments.

If you color your hair, we sincerely hope you're having it done in a salon. The risks of doing it yourself are extensive, particularly on fragile hair. The bottom line is that box color is like a box of chocolates: you never know what you're going to get. The odds of the shade turning out like the photo on the box are remote. Your hair's porosity, texture, current color, and condition all come into play, so you and a friend can both use the same brand of chestnut brown and end up with completely different results. What's more, the formula is one-dimensional, so your hair color will be monochromatic and flat—which also translates to old-looking. We urge you to spring for a pro who's gone to cosmetology school and knows how to apply color, add highlights, and keep your hair in the best possible condition.

If you've opted to let your hair take its natural course, you've probably noticed that the gray is frizzier than your original color and has a tendency to turn yellow. Regular use of a moisturizing shampoo and conditioner will help with the wiriness, and a purple shampoo and/or conditioner (also ideal for blondes) will neutralize any yellow tones.

MAKEUP

While we've frequently mentioned that the internet is a valuable tool for accessing lots of useful information, our research shows that it's the worst place to go for makeup advice. The sites we visited contradicted each other with such consistency that we knew we had to go to the true experts: the makeup professionals of Los Angeles.

Jamie Haynes is the founder of *Rouge Artists*, an agency that represents a world-class roster of entertainment professionals, including renowned makeup artists. She was kind enough to put us in touch with some talented women who know everything there is to know about putting your best face forward. They regularly work with celebrities—including those of a certain age—and here's what they have to say:

Elan Bongiorno, founder of Enjoué Beauté and Daytime Emmy Award nominee for Outstanding Makeup: Says Elan, "Cosmetics are an everyday essential—an instant lift. If you look good, you feel good, and that is empowering. Makeup to me is magical."

Elan is a firm believer in the power of drinking lots of water to hydrate and plump the skin. While it's an important step for all women, it's especially critical for women over fifty.

She also recommends using a multi-purpose BB cream to streamline your beauty regimen. Short for "beauty balm," a BB cream does the work of a moisturizer, primer, sunscreen, concealer, and light foundation—boosted by skin-loving ingredients to protect and nourish. In one step, it evens out skin tone and gives an instant brightening effect, so whether you're a fan of makeup or prefer absolute simplicity, a BB cream just might be your perfect solution. (We don't know about you, but we're rushing out to buy some now.)

As women age, under-eye darkness can become increasingly problematic. Elan suggests using a concealer to brighten things up—and to look about ten years younger. Make sure to apply it on the inner corner of the eye as well, since this is the area where skin tends to be the darkest. Depending upon your skin tone, use a salmon or a honey shade. If you're unsure, visit just about any department-store makeup counter for color advice.

Dark eyeshadows are not kind to older women, so use them sparingly. Start with a warm taupe color in the crease and a light, satin-finish shade on the lid to brighten the eyes, then smudge a darker shade into the lash line to make your eyes pop.

The thick brows of youth are as far behind us as our bikini days, but there's no need to go through life with a barely-there look. Choose a brow powder that most closely matches your natural brow color and use it to fill in any sparse areas with light, feathery strokes. Then apply a darker shade to the arch for an instant brow lift.

Skin tone and lip pigment fade as we get older, so it's important to use more vibrant cheek and lip colors. This doesn't mean grandma's bright-red rouge circles, but rather a light application of a complementary color that will give you a healthy glow. Avoid brown lip shades, which do not provide the contrast you're seeking. Instead, look for lip colors with a blue undertone, which will help make teeth look whiter and brighter.

Kerry Herta, makeup department head of Colour Box Makeup Studios and Emmy Award nominee: "A radiant glow is the sign of being healthy and vibrant," states Kerry, "and the right makeup can reflect that radiance." She suggests avoiding dry powders, which can look dull and lifeless on the skin, and opting instead for a moisturizing foundation with light-diffusing qualities. Cream blushes are an easy way to keep the skin looking soft and healthy while providing a pop of color, and if you put nothing else on your face, at least brighten those cheeks.

Kerry recommends curling the lashes to give the eye a more open and fresh look. If your mascara tends to roam all over the place, apply it to the top lashes only or use a waterproof formula. If you don't like the dryness of a waterproof mascara but want the wearability, use non-waterproof to get your desired look, then finish it off with a swipe of waterproof to seal it. Gel eyeliners are a great way to add definition around the eye, and their formulas are long lasting.

And here's the tip we've been waiting for: how to remove tenacious eye makeup at the end of the day. Kerry suggests using a micellar solution, which gently draws out impurities without the need for rubbing. Most of these cleansers don't even need to be rinsed with water, and they can be found at any drug store.

Lip color is another way to look fresh and vibrant as you age, and a bold color can be very empowering. A longwearing cream formula is a better choice than matte to keep with that radiant look. To prevent lipstick from running into fine lines around the mouth, outline the lips with a pencil in the same shade as the lipstick, then blend it all around the lip. Lip pencils have more pigment than lipsticks, so they'll stay on longer and help avoid fading and smearing. If you want your lips to appear fuller, use a pencil to subtly overdraw your lips by tracing just the very edge of the outside border. It's best to start from the outer corner and work inward.

Eye shadow is a fun way to express yourself and create a more dressed-up, glamorous look. Always put the lightest color—cream and peachy shades work well—near the lash line to make the eyes appear more open. (Danged gravity!) Avoid shimmers in the crease of the eye or under the brow bone. Kerry is a big fan of layering products for optimum wear: using a cream base on the lid and applying shadow over it.

Finish your face with a matte highlighter on the cheekbones, just above your blush. Anything that reflects or diffuses light will give you a soft, youthful look. Highlighter is an easy way to contour, especially if you add a swipe to the bridge of your nose and the middle of your forehead.

To provide you with the greatest scope of information, we also tapped into the expertise of other beauty experts.

Julie Morgan, founder of Foxyfleet, a talented group of makeup artists on both coasts: Julie knows from working with clients over fifty that skin can look dull and lackluster as both the exfoliation process and circulation slow down. To regain that youthful glow, she suggests utilizing a bit of fingertip massage to thoroughly cleanse skin and remove makeup. Massage and light tapping when applying skincare products are beneficial, as well.

Mature skin looks best when the tone is evened out, and a CC (color correcting) cream does precisely that. In addition to blurring discoloration, it also serves as a primer, broad-spectrum sunscreen, and foundation. Julie explains that both CC and BB creams help skin look younger, and many of them self-adjust to match the precise color of your skin. She recommends those made by Erborian, a Korean and French beauty collaboration.

Julie also touts the magic-wand effect of a concealer pencil to lift shadowed areas through the T-zone, highlight the inner corner of the eye, and create a more voluminous lip. Her preferred brands include Julie Hewitt and Cargo.

Blush can turn back the clock by adding youthful vibrancy to the skin. Julie suggests having fun with it and trying different shades and textures to achieve the look you want.

"I like popsicle brights for spring/summer and mulberry tones for fall/winter," she says. For the most long-lasting effect, sweep a powder blush over a cream one. The products that are regularly at her fingertips include Last Looks by Juice Beauty, which boasts organic formulas; NARS Liquid Blush; Bobbi Brown Cheek Glow Palettes; and Jouer Mineral Powder Blush. Her signature application is to create a soft halo of blush in a C shape from the apple of the cheek through the temple.

Julie warns that a brow powder or pencil that is too dark and harsh can pull the eye downward, so stick to more natural shades. And, of course, a little cleanup of unwanted hairs and fuzz can brighten and lift the eye. Stay away from shimmery shadows, and instead opt for a cream consistency. To enhance and brighten the eyes, consider navy, charcoal, or violet liner tucked into the lash line instead of the more traditional black. Softly blend a medium-shade shadow on the hooded area of the eye to create a lifted lid.

As a finishing touch, Julie suggests spritzing your face and décolletage with rose water, which gives a hydrated and soft, luminous look to makeup.

Amy Nadine Clement, co-founder of The Beauty Department: Amy's first word of advice is to stay away from any makeup that has a high shimmer, which could highlight wrinkles. She, too, suggests wearing bright lipstick and avoiding dark eyeshadows. Her recommended routine for baby boomers is fill in the brow, line the lip, and contour the jawline—her regimen for Susan Sarandon. And if it's good enough for the lovely Ms. Sarandon, it's good enough for us!

Matthew Muellenhoff, DO, FAOCD, FAAD

Dr. Matthew Muellenhoff is the founder and medical director of SIERRADERM in Grass Valley, California. He is board certified in dermatology, a Fellow of the American Osteopathic College of Dermatology, and a member of the American Academy of Dermatology. He shares with us an abundance of information on facial skincare, body skincare, non-invasive cosmetic procedures, and body contouring for the over-fifty woman.

FACIAL SKINCARE

AUTHORS: *What type of daily skincare regimen do you recommend to women over fifty?*

DR. MUELLENHOFF: Protect in the morning and correct at night—that's my mantra. Start your day with a gentle cleanser, followed by an antioxidant and topped off with a moisturizing sunscreen. I am not a proponent of toners, because I just don't think they do a whole lot. Makeup can go on after your sunscreen. I am a fan of mineral-based makeup lines, because they don't include preservatives, chemical dyes, or fragrances.

In the evening, consider exfoliation with an alpha-hydroxy acid cleanser and some form of vitamin A topical, such as tretinoin, retinaldehyde, or retinol. This is a good time to incorporate more than one active ingredient, and layering is okay. Skin tends to dry with age, so if those products aren't moisturizing enough, finish with a moisturizer that leaves your skin feeling replenished.

AUTHORS: *Are department-store products as effective as those available through a dermatologist?*

DR. MUELLENHOFF: The anti-aging skincare market is huge, and many companies make lofty claims about the efficacy and superiority of their products—whether they're true or not. By comparison, the prescription-strength anti-aging products commonly recommended by dermatologists are targeted and proven to be very effective. Common examples of these are tretinoin, a cream used for wrinkle reduction, and skin-lightening agents recommended for brown spots. Additionally, a dermatologist can tailor a skin regimen incorporating both prescription and quality non-prescription products that focus on a woman's unique skin characteristics. In my opinion: advantage dermatologist.

I don't mean to be unilaterally critical of department-store products. Some are quite similar to what you might find in a dermatology office: a high-quality, cosmetically elegant sunscreen or a hyaluronic acid-based moisturizer. Perhaps the biggest problem with shopping for skincare in a retail store is that there is often a lot of buzz or hype that can lead shoppers to the impulse buy. Just remember that the devil is in the details. Look for actual concentrations of active ingredient on the bottle. More of something is not always better, but it certainly will steer you away from products that make claims but don't have the power to deliver. Compare different brands. One may list a concentration while another doesn't. Department stores offer a lot of variety, and that gives you the opportunity to shop around.

An additional word of caution: there is no one cream suited for every skin type. Feel it. Smell it. Try it on your skin. One of the more expensive anti-aging products on the market smells like burnt tires. Finding out you are repulsed by your $250 facial cream is a bummer—let alone that it might be too heavy for your skin and cause you to break out. It never hurts to ask for samples. Doing a bit of homework always pays off—or work with a dermatologist to find what is best for you.

AUTHORS: *What about drugstore products? Are they any good?*

DR. MUELLENHOFF: Yes, some are, and I especially like the ceramide-based moisturizers. Ceramides improve skin barrier function and the ability of the skin to retain moisture. These moisturizing creams are geared toward dry to very dry skin types, and also offer alternative lotion preparation for those who are less dry but still would like a quality moisturizer. Example brands that have ceramide-based lines include Cerave, Cetaphil, and Eucerin.

AUTHORS: *What are the ingredients a woman should look for when deciding what creams, lotions, etc. to buy?*

DR. MUELLENHOFF: Skin aging is a host of losses and gains: loss in volume, tone, and collagen; gains in spots, growths, and wrinkles. The usual conversation focuses on how to get back the losses and get rid of the gains, but what is often not addressed is how to preserve what is still there. What happened between ages thirty and fifty might be hair-raising, but consider from fifty to seventy.

As women age, I think it is a critical step to take a close look at prevention in addition to correction. Religious sunscreen use and adding a topical antioxidant that can boost protection are a solid foundation to any skincare program. Antioxidants are widely utilized in both over-the-counter and physician-dispensed product lines. My favorites include the vitamin C/vitamin E combination products, and I really like the newer formulas that offer extended release. We are exposed to sun, pollutants, and various oxidative stressors all day. Why not have protective action all day, as well?

I often recommend at least some form of vitamin A topical, such as tretinoin, retinaldehyde, and retinol. Call me old-fashioned, but topical vitamin A is well studied, proven to be effective, and readily available. It regulates and normalizes skin turnover, reduces risk of skin cancer and pre-cancer, evens skin tone, and reduces wrinkles. Sign me up, right? Well...not so fast. It can also turn you red and peely and can make you sensitive to the sun. Picking the right concentration can help avoid this, or you can try diluting it with your moisturizer or skipping a day between applications.

I am a big proponent of zinc-based sunscreens. Most sunscreens are often a hodge-podge of different chemicals that, when added together, make up "broad UV spectrum coverage." Zinc, on the other hand, has the advantage of broad protection across the UV spectrum all on its own. I liken it to this analogy: if you are going out in the rain, do you want to carry a bunch of little umbrellas or one big one? EltaMD is my go-to line of sunscreens featuring a variety of zinc-based products for just about every skin type. Yes, zinc can get "ghosty," especially at higher concentrations, but formulations have improved. Now zinc can be invisible when applied, or tinted like a foundation. For oily or acne-prone skin, I love the Elta Clear, since it is absolutely sheer and can reduce some redness in the skin, as well.

Hyaluronic acid (HA) is very popular right now, and can be found in many anti-aging products, moisturizers, serums, and BB creams. HA is a natural component of deeper skin that surrounds collagen bundles, and it is also what we inject as a cosmetic filler for wrinkle reduction and facial sculpting. When applied topically to the skin, it brings water to the surface, effectively plumping the skin to soften the appearance of wrinkles and improve texture.

Growth factors: this is an exciting and controversial area in skincare, but I do not recommend it for those over fifty who have a lot of sun damage or history of skin cancer. Growth factors—which are naturally present in skin cells but decrease as we age—signal skin cells to grow and divide, produce collagen, and can even accelerate wound healing. There are many different growth factors—EGF, TGF, VEGF, the list goes on—that signal cells to do different things.

Because they can work synergistically, products often contain more than one. Some dermatologists feel that growth factors cannot penetrate the skin when applied topically, and therefore have minimal benefit. Others, including myself, feel that growth factors could stimulate bad or damaged cells to grow just as easily as good cells, potentially leading to accelerated skin-cancer growth. Since skin cancer is so common in over-fifty skin anyway, it just doesn't seem to be a good fit. A viable alternative is a brand-new product line that signals undamaged stem cells hiding in your hair follicles to grow, divide, and produce new pristine skin cells. This gives a whole new meaning to skin renewal.

AUTHORS: *In your opinion, what constitutes healthy skin on an older woman?*

DR. MUELLENHOFF: Healthy skin is a reflection of overall health. Getting restful and adequate sleep, eating smart, not smoking, and having a healthy relationship with the sun (avoiding excessive exposure and using sun protection) are all areas to focus on for good skin health.

OVERALL BODY SKINCARE

AUTHORS: *Explain why a woman should have a visual body scan (moles, freckles, new spots and growths, etc.).*

DR.MUELLENHOFF: Simply put, skin cancer can affect any age. We all have spots, growths, moles. Completely clear skin is actually pretty rare, especially as we age. Being mindful of what is on you is a good first step. How can you know if something new has developed if you don't know what was already there?

AUTHORS: *How often should this be done?*

DR. MUELLENHOFF: I recommend that everyone over fifty should get annual skin exams.

FACIAL COSMETIC PROCEDURES

AUTHORS: *What are the advantages of non-invasive procedures, such as Botox® and fillers?*

DR. MUELLENHOFF: I would say non-invasive is key. Downtime is minimal with these procedures. Risk is low. Satisfaction is high. I also like the fact that Botox and fillers are not permanent. Your face will change over time—guaranteed. Being able to adjust my placement and dosage of these products allows me to customize a treatment plan that works for that patient at that moment.

AUTHORS: *Which non-invasive procedures are most effective?*

DR. MUELLENHOFF: I am so amazed at what can be done with combinations of fillers and Botox right now. The different products available allow me to offer very natural results. As a whole, I believe cosmetic injectors have moved away from simply filling a line or giving patients the "frozen" look. Also, what's good for a lip is different than for a cheek. It is not uncommon to discuss a few different products with a patient or to layer Botox in an area where I did some filler to enhance an effect.

AUTHORS: *How long do they last?*

DR. MUELLENHOFF: The current neuromodulators on the U.S. market (Botox, Xeomin, Dysport) generally last four months. We are eagerly awaiting the approval of a new product that has been shown to last six months. Fillers can last from six months up to two years, depending on which product is used.

AUTHORS: *Are there downsides?*

DR. MUELLENHOFF: I believe the biggest downside to any aesthetic procedure is the unknown risk. No woman wants a droopy brow or a lump in her skin. Experienced injectors can certainly reduce some of those risks, but we cannot eliminate them completely. Thankfully, complications are extremely rare, and we have ways to minimize or fix them.

What I find equally concerning for patients is the fear of an unnatural result. This is where the initial consultation is so important. Each individual is unique and has different goals, desires, and anatomy. My job is to understand those and match the proper procedure—be it Botox, laser, filler, or a combination—to best address the concern. Good communication is key. Pain from procedures can also be a concern, but with refined techniques, integrated numbing agents, and downsized Botox needles, I find this to be less and less of an issue.

AUTHORS: *What happens if a woman who's been using Botox and fillers stops doing the procedures?*

DR. MUELLENHOFF: These products have a lifespan, so when that lifespan ends, the effect disappears. Someone who has faithfully been using Botox and filler for ten years and then suddenly stops is still ten years older. The absence of these products may make that seem more dramatic, but that's Mother Nature's fault, not the Botox or filler.

BODY-BEAUTIFYING PROCEDURES

AUTHORS: *Are there any effective procedures for crepey and/or sagging skin on the body?*

DR. MUELLENHOFF: Yes, the body contouring market is booming. There are many options, but all of them generally work by heating the deeper tissues to cause tightening. I think results can be very impressive to very subtle, and often the photos advertised show the most dramatic results. Get a good idea of what an average correction would be so you know what to expect and to determine if it's a good value for you.

AUTHORS: *Are there any new procedures on the market that older women might want to explore?*

DR. MUELLENHOFF: The fat-dissolving market is a newer development. These are devices that freeze or heat fat, causing it to disappear. CoolSculpting® and SculpSure® are two devices that seem to be leading the charge. This is not a replacement for liposuction, but it can address love handles, saddle bags, and other more focused areas of fat that we would love to see a little less of.

ACTION STEPS

I am willing to take stock of my appearance and try to improve the image I present to the world by taking the following action. (Check all that apply.)

I will do what I can to establish and embrace a style that feels comfortable to me.	
I will wear clothes that look good on me, and I will ask a fashionable friend or a pro for help if I can't figure it out on my own.	
I will take stock of my wardrobe and get rid of items that are unflattering, outdated, or don't fit.	
I will get a haircut that's appropriate for my age, coloring, and hair type.	
If I choose to go gray (and that's a perfectly fine option), I'll get a good haircut.	

Chapter 7

Learning—It's Not Just for Kids

"Learning is not attained by chance. It must be sought for with ardor and attended to with diligence."—Abigail Adams, former First Lady of the United States

We've all heard the stories about the grandmother who received her high-school diploma at sixty-four and went on to get a college degree, graduating at the top of her class at the age of sixty-eight. For women who came of age in the 1960s, the importance of having a good education was a mantra repeated in households across the nation. After high school, we had two choices: go to college to meet the man of our dreams and get married, or go to college and become a nurse or a teacher—a great choice until we stopped working to raise a family. At that point, the focus was on the kids: helping them with homework, driving them to music lessons, and picking them up from after-school activities. Many of us willingly gave up our lives to raise our children and support our husbands.

Some of us went on to graduate school, law school, or medical school, finding professions that sustained us and allowed us to have the freedom and flexibility previously available only to men. In spite of advancing education and training, however, many women born in 1946 (the earliest boomers) likely experienced the rampant sexism in the workplace that was depicted in the "Mad Men" television series.

And then 1967 brought the summer of love and everything changed. For the first time, everyone—especially women—rebelled against the establishment. We burned our bras, spoke out against the Vietnam War, took control of abortion legislation, entered the political scene, and danced naked at Woodstock. With role models like political activists Gloria

Steinem and Angela Davis, we acted out and demanded equal rights. We were busy women making it happen.

While our generation became highly educated, the concept of lifelong learning didn't appear until the dawning of the age of the internet. Suddenly, information was available at our fingertips. Staying current with news, politics, films, books—just about anything, for that matter—was more possible than ever before. The point: there is no excuse not to learn something new every single day. We've come a long way, baby.

Okay, so maybe you have some catching up to do. It doesn't matter, because it's never too late to seize the day and broaden your horizons. Why? For starters, learning for the sake of learning is good for the psyche and good for the soul. What's more, expanded knowledge helps stimulate conversation when you get together with your buddies, so you'll have something to talk about besides your grandkids, your aches and pains, or your upcoming surgery.

Even if you haven't read anything more challenging than the Sue Grafton series in the last several years, it's time to change your ways and add some educational material to the list. This chapter will give you lots of wonderful ideas for stimulating your brain and making an effort to keep up with younger generations.

Before we go any further, let's see where you stand.

I am a voracious reader of both fiction and nonfiction. I'm in the Mensa society (or should be!) and could win "Jeopardy" with the greatest of ease.									
1	2	3	4	5	6	7	8	9	10

I have many interests, and I regularly read magazines and journals on a variety of topics.									
1	2	3	4	5	6	7	8	9	10

I spend about an hour each day reading new information online.									
1	2	3	4	5	6	7	8	9	10

I often enroll in online classes as well as classes at my local community college.									
1	2	3	4	5	6	7	8	9	10

I frequently visit my local public library.									
1	2	3	4	5	6	7	8	9	10

My idea of the perfect vacation is to visit a place where I can learn about other cultures.									
1	2	3	4	5	6	7	8	9	10

If you're already reading nonfiction on your Kindle, keeping pace with your local political candidates, perusing the internet for home-improvement tutorials before calling a plumber or electrician, learning to cook exotic foods, and watching YouTube videos about the destinations on your bucket list, you've mastered the art of lifelong learning. However, if you aren't quite up to speed, this chapter will help you discover some options that are at your disposal.

There's no doubt that learning something new will help you become a more interesting person—the person you were before things like marriage, kids, and career defined you, diverting attention from your own personal interests. That woman is still in there some-where, eager to break out and embrace life. You may just need to rattle her a bit.

As we get older, many of us fall into the habit of resting on our laurels. We are content with previous successes and don't do very much to keep the momentum going. When the good old days becomes the primary topic of conversation, it's like watching "Seinfeld" rer‹...›—they're still funny the first few times, but you eventually have to change the channel.

Odds are, your family and friends have heard the stories of your accomplishments so many times that they could recite them along with you. It doesn't matter how amazing you were back in the day. This is today, and it's time to talk about something new.

That doesn't mean engaging in a lively discussion about your failing health and stamina. It doesn't mean touting the antics of your eight-year-old granddaughter, who is brilliant, talented, and adorable—just like her remarkable mother whom you raised alone while putting yourself through grad school. Enough. You are better than this, and learning something new is the best way we know to become interesting once again.

Now it's time to figure out what you want to learn and how best to go about it. This will be difficult if you haven't studied since high school or college or practiced a musical instrument since junior high, but it can be done.

PURSUING A DEGREE

If college wasn't part of your past, you can make it part of your future—and you don't even have to set foot in a classroom. There's a website dedicated to affordable online colleges,[24] and the focus is on schools that offer academic excellence at a manageable price tag. You can earn a degree in a diversity of specialties, such as education, business, healthcare, organizational leadership, or criminal justice. Courses are delivered through a variety of platforms, including Blackboard, Skype, online discussions, and email.

TAKING A CLASS

If you simply want to take a class or two without completing a degree, the possibilities are endless. Most community colleges offer adult education, and you can learn about subjects such as creative arts, food and drink, technology, and travel. You can also find a host of free online courses offered by prestigious universities at edx.org, which partners with schools that include Harvard, MIT, Berkeley, Boston University, Caltech, Sorbonne Universités, and the University of Hong Kong. Classes run the gamut from *Cybersecurity Fundamentals* to *Cloud Computing*—from *How to Write a Novel* to *Italian Language and Culture*—from *Making Sense of Climate Science Denial* to *How Politicians Debate*. All you need to do is find one that appeals to you, sign up, and prepare to be the most dazzling guest at the next dinner party.

PODCASTS, PAPERS, AND BOOKS

Of course, you don't have to go to a college or university to learn something new. Your local library offers a wealth of opportunities with a selection of memoirs, autobiographies, nonfiction, blogs, magazines, and research papers on just about any topic that interests you. While you're there, ask about joining a nonfiction book club.

If you learn best by listening, give podcasts, radio shows, and audio books a try. Visit npr.org/podcasts to access categories that include news and politics, religion and spirituality, and society and culture. Log on to learnoutloud.com, where you'll find a directory of more than 2,000 podcasts. If you're budget conscious and find the idea of free audio books appealing, check out thebalance.com for thousands of titles.

If you learn best by seeing, video education might be just right for you. Openculture.com offers free online video courses from top universities, addressing topics such as art history, mythology, film, and cooking. Another great source of video learning is TED—which stands for technology, entertainment, and design—a nonprofit that began as a conference in 1984. TED Talks are videos from expert speakers on education, business, science, technology, and creativity. More than 2,400 talks are available in 100+ languages at ted.com/talks, and all are eighteen minutes long or less.

BUT WAIT—THERE'S MORE

Need additional inspiration? Try expanding your knowledge on a familiar topic. For example, take your love of photography up a notch by learning Photoshop, or sign up for a class in digital photography. Elevate your scarf-knitting skills by making a sweater with cables and multiple colors of yarn. If you write poetry, try your hand at short stories, or research and write an article on a topic that intrigues you. If you're an artist who's always enjoyed painting, take a class in sculpting or calligraphy. If you play the guitar, add violin or cello lessons. If you have an ear for languages and already speak more than one, expand your repertoire with Japanese or Farsi.

Another option is to try something you've never done before: reading music, playing bridge, changing the oil in your car, or growing vegetables. Learn CPR or American Sign Language. Get certified as a scuba diver or take up birdwatching. Take a stand-up comedy class or learn how to install a wood floor. Instead of going to the gym, get your exercise by learning to dance salsa or tango, or take a class in self-defense. Have the travel bug? Plan a trip to a place you've never been. In preparation, learn everything you can about the culture, history, customs, and language. Master at least ten basic phrases. Start a travel blog. When you return, learn the software and put together a slide show.

If you're mostly in your head, step outside of your comfort zone and explore something physical, like yoga, tai chi, or qigong. If you spend most of your free time on the treadmill, tackle something more cerebral like sacred geometry or meditation.

Whatever type of new learning you decide to undertake, keep in mind that you're not being graded or judged. If you hear your eighth-grade teacher's voice telling you you'll never be good at French or English Lit or PE, tell that imaginary nitwit to shut the fuck up. Don't let criticism and judgment thwart your efforts or undermine your progress before you begin.

And while we're on the subject, make sure to cut out any negative self-talk. You're not too old, too tired, or too dumb to learn something new. If you're worried about what your kids, husband, or best friend might say about your recent interest—and you know that a negative comment is likely to stop you in your tracks—then keep it to yourself. Perfection is not the goal. Instead, the objective here is to broaden your horizons.

At this stage in life, the courage to take chances may be lacking. If this is you, ask yourself what you have to lose. So often, women put their needs on the back burner and let them stay there to simmer and eventually evaporate. Taking time out to learn something new—to be open to new concepts and ideas that could potentially change your life by expanding your social circle—is one of the best things you can do for yourself and your loved ones.

ENHANCING MEMORY

As an added bonus, learning something new can improve your long-term memory. Fear of memory loss often goes hand in hand with the aging process, so it's heartening to know that you can exercise your brain so you don't leave your car keys in the freezer or your hat in the linen closet.

Research conducted by Dr. Denise Park,[25] a neuroscientist at the University of Texas at Dallas, concluded that picking up a challenging hobby improves long-term memory far better than watching movies, reminiscing about past vacations, listening to classical music, playing easy games, or working puzzles. According to Park, "Only people who learned a new skill had significant gains." What's more, those gains remained a year later when the 200 participants were retested.

Park isn't alone. Research on how we learn is abundant, and much of it concludes that learning complex tasks causes neurons in the brain to forge new connections that make the mind more flexible and powerful. An article that appeared on the Science News for Students website[26] states, "As we learn something new, cells that send and receive information about the task become more and more efficient. It takes less effort for them to signal the next cell about what's going on. In a sense, the neurons become wired together."

While we're on the subject of brain function, we'd like to mention our good friend the hippocampus, the area of the brain associated with memory. Shaped like a horseshoe, its structure is divided into two halves that lie on each side of the brain just above the ears. The good news: now you know where your hippocampus is. The bad news: it's not as big as it used to be.

The brain shrinks with age, and the hippocampus does so at an even faster rate. So what can you do about it? In an article that appeared in Harvard Health Publications, author Heidi Godman states, "In a study done at the University of British Columbia, researchers found that regular aerobic exercise, the kind that gets your heart and your sweat glands pumping, appears to boost the size of the hippocampus."[27] With this in mind (no pun intended), perhaps your learning something new might include dancing, water aerobics, roller skating, or tennis.

If trying to figure out what to learn seems overwhelming, try this exercise. As you go through your typical day, pay attention to the situations that cause you confusion or lack of clarity. Do you dread April because you don't understand taxes? Consider taking that H&R Block class you've joked about. Perhaps you've never paid attention to local, national, or global politics and you'd like to join the conversation. Make a personal commitment to read at least two news magazines with differing points of view. Are you baffled by new technology—afraid to buy a new TV or computer because of the learning curve? Go ahead and purchase whatever you've been avoiding and then read the manual (we know it sounds awful, but that's what it's there for) or take a computer class at the library.

Learning something new doesn't have to be a huge undertaking. It could be as simple as becoming a news junkie, expanding your vocabulary, or picking up interesting facts you can use to impress your friends. We've mentioned a few internet sites you can peruse to learn a little or a lot, but we've barely touched the surface. If you'd like more options, just Google "learn something new." You'll be amazed at how much pops up.

Natalie Hoogasian

Natalie met her husband when she was seventeen. By the time she was twenty, she was married and pregnant. Like so many women, she went from her family's home to her husband's home with little thought of independence. In spite of a domineering spouse and a growing family, she managed to hold various part- and full-time positions at The Emporium, a department store in San Francisco. When she decided that she wanted to drive, she had to fight with her husband for permission to get her license—particularly ironic in light of the fact that he was a driver's education instructor.

After twenty-two years of marriage, much of which was spent discouraging his wife's ambitions, Natalie's husband announced his plan to quit teaching. The ultimate blow was delivered when he told her she would have to get a "real" job if they were to maintain their lifestyle.

At the age of forty-two, she set out to turn her clerk positions at The Emporium into a career. She boldly asked for, and was given, a promotion to manager of the fine jewelry department. In charge of a staff of thirty people, she began to flourish with self-confidence. Three years later, she ended her marriage.

Natalie eventually accepted the position of fine jewelry manager and buyer at Saks Fifth Avenue in San Francisco. She worked in that capacity for twenty-one years, taking twice-yearly buying trips throughout Europe. It was during her travels that she developed an interest in photography.

"When I was married," recalls Natalie, "there was always a camera in the home, but it never dawned on me to pick it up. I could have been capturing the lives of my children on film for all those years! If only I'd had the confidence back then to do something that was fulfilling to *me*."

At the age of sixty-five, Natalie retired from the retail business. It was the first time in more than forty years that her life was truly her own, and she relished the thought of having zero responsibility to anyone or anything but herself.

"I realized I could sit at home and watch movies all day if I wanted to. That feeling of absolute freedom lasted about two weeks—and then it turned to acute boredom."

She decided to focus her energies on photography to see if she could turn a hobby into a new career. After renting a studio in a building inhabited exclusively by artists—"I thought the Muse would be more likely to visit in an environment like that"—she began to explore opportunities for work. For the next several years, she managed to combine her love of travel with her growing skill behind the lens. Eventually, she booked a trip to Egypt with a group whose purpose was to experience the spiritual aspects of the country.

To Natalie, the most exciting component of the adventure was access to temples and monuments that were otherwise closed to the public. Camera in hand, she would quietly shoot these venerable spaces while others around her meditated and prayed. It was on this trip that she met a poet who shared her spiritual sensibilities, and the two women decided to collaborate on a book of poems and photos.

"Once we were satisfied with the shape the book was taking, we started sending query letters to literary agents and publishers. With no one to guide us, we were operating entirely in the dark. Oh, we read books on the subject. We learned what to do and what not to do. We were educated on the importance of including the sacred self-addressed stamped envelope. But we simply weren't prepared for the rejections. Over the course of the next several months, we accumulated dozens of thanks-but-no-thanks letters—but we refused to quit.

"Self-publishing seemed like an alternative worth exploring, so I attended a very informative lecture on the subject. It sounded like the perfect solution until the speaker mentioned storage. A coffee-table art book would have to be kept in a climate-controlled space to avoid extreme temperatures that could ruin it. *Great*, I thought. *Not only do we have to pay to print the book, we have to pay to store it, too.* And then he talked about marketing. It would be necessary for us to promote and sell the book—something we knew nothing about. I left the lecture feeling overwhelmed and disillusioned.

"A few weeks later, while attending a book-signing in San Francisco, I met the vice president of a small boutique publisher that specializes in fine art books. Of course I told him about my book—I told anyone who would listen about my book!—and he politely suggested that I call him when it was completed.

"As soon as the final photo was matched to a poem, I made that call. We set up a meeting for him to review our work, and we were as nervous as schoolgirls when we entered the conference room. By the time the meeting ended, we were clutching book contracts to review with our attorney.

"Five months after I turned 71, *In This My Beautiful Egypt* was published."

ACTION STEPS

I am willing to keep learning and become a more knowledgeable and informed person by taking the following action. (Check all that apply.)	
I will spend some time every day reading about current events.	
I will look for, join, or start a nonfiction book club.	
I will research a topic of interest every day.	
I will look for lectures and events in my community that will give me something to talk about.	
I will research online and community classes that interest me.	
I will commit to being a more interesting person.	

Chapter 8

Tapping into Generosity

"Giving back makes you happier by both giving you a sense of purpose and helping to put your problems in perspective."
— Karen Salmansohn, American self-help author

According to psychologist Paul Bloom, "We are constituted so that simple acts of kindness, such as giving to charity or expressing gratitude, have a positive effect on our long-term moods. The key to the happy life, it seems, is the good life: a life with sustained relationships, challenging work, and connections to community."

Once you hit retirement age—and before, if you are able—giving back is one way to remain viable and connected. It doesn't matter if you're giving time, money, or your expertise; sharing what you have will make you feel good.

We encourage you to look for opportunities to be generous in a variety of ways and as often as possible. It's easy to believe that spending the better part of your adult life working and/or raising a family gives you the right to be (dare we say it?) selfish at this point, but we're asking you to rethink this concept.

Perhaps giving back is already a part of your lifestyle, but if it's not, we'll help you discover how easy it is to make contributions. First, let's see where you stand.

I regularly donate to charity, and most of my family members and friends say I'm a very giving person.

1	2	3	4	5	6	7	8	9	10

I offer my time freely and always feel good about it.

1	2	3	4	5	6	7	8	9	10

Kind words, hugs, and showing appreciation and gratitude come easily to me.

1	2	3	4	5	6	7	8	9	10

I have no problem finding ways to be helpful to family members and friends.

1	2	3	4	5	6	7	8	9	10

I seek out ways to give back to my community.

1	2	3	4	5	6	7	8	9	10

If I see a situation where I can be of help—and I have the time and energy to jump in—I volunteer without waiting to be asked.

1	2	3	4	5	6	7	8	9	10

If you regularly give to others without feeling depleted or resentful, we applaud you and hope you'll continue. You can't take it with you, and it's much better to deal with your worldly possessions while you're still in the world and capable of managing your loot. Besides, you'll be a wonderful role model for your kids and for the rest of us. If you're having trouble expanding your giving energy to include others, this chapter will give you some suggestions on ways you can make a difference.

If you were raised in a climate of giving—with parents who donated to the March of Dimes, put coins in the collection basket at church, bought Girl Scout cookies every year, or planted trees in Israel—sharing what you have probably comes naturally. You understand what the Buddha meant when he said, "Generosity brings happiness at every stage of its expression. We experience joy in forming the intention to be generous. We experience joy in the actual act of giving something. And we experience joy in remembering the fact that we have given."

If, on the other hand, you were raised in a household that was scrimping and saving just to put food on the table, being generous with your hard-earned cash might not be part of your mindset. However, clinging to a childhood notion that there isn't enough—if you truly have plenty as an adult—serves no purpose other than to make you seem miserly. Having a bundle in the bank might be what gives you peace of mind and allows you to sleep at night. Understood. But unless you're planning to be buried like an Egyptian Pharaoh—with all of your prized possessions tucked into your tomb—consider giving some of it away now and enjoy a new peace of mind: the joy of giving.

The indigenous people of the Pacific Northwest Coast of Canada and the United States have a ceremony called a potlatch, where people give away their most useful or valued possessions. The ceremony teaches people to share what they most value, and it is considered a disgrace to give away used or broken items or to expect anything in return. The point of the ceremony is to share what you can, give away something that can be helpful to another, and to let go of holding on to things.

Just for the heck of it, play around with giving. The next time your daughter comments on something of yours that she loves—a painting, an antique brooch, a sweater—give it to her. Then stop and observe the joy she experiences from receiving an unexpected gift. At the same time, notice the feelings that come up for you. Being generous creates a win-win situation, benefitting both the giver and the receiver.

For many of us, a more practical, dialed-back approach to giving might be necessary. The internet is filled with articles on the legalities and nuances of giving gifts to your heirs, and they address strategies such as tax-free gifting: tax-exempt ways to help cover your child's or grandchild's medical, dental, and tuition expenses, and to fund college savings plans.

MONETARY CONTRIBUTIONS

If you've been fortunate enough to make more money than you could possibly spend and need a charitable contribution on your tax return, the National Center for Charitable Statistics points out that there are more than 1.5 million nonprofit organizations registered in the U.S. that you can choose from. These include public charities, private foundations, chambers of commerce, fraternal organizations, and civic leagues. Of the many ways to give, a monetary contribution is the easiest. All it requires is writing a check, dropping cash in a collection basket, or, if you are truly blessed with abundance, adding an endowment to your will.

NON-CASH DONATIONS

If you've been amassing stuff for decades and have a garage or attic filled with things you haven't touched in ages, you might be able to put them to good use by donating them to a nonprofit. As we mentioned in the chapter on behaviors, getting rid of unnecessary items is a great way to tidy up your life. It's also a great way to help others who might benefit from your castoffs, so the advantages are twofold. If you're having trouble letting go, it might be time to rethink the reasons why.

I might use this again some day... Seriously? And when is the last time you used that pasta maker? If it's been untouched for years, give it to the hospice thrift store. It will likely be snatched up by someone who'd love to try making fettuccini from scratch, and the money they pay for it will go toward helping people in need.

It belonged to my great-grandmother... We promise you she will not roll over in her grave if you donate her china to The Salvation Army. If sentiment is what's holding you back, take a photo of the dishes and stick it in your family album.

These clothes cost me a small fortune... Sure, you spent a lot of money on the suits that were your daily wardrobe when you were working in corporate America, but it's unlikely that you have any need for them now. Give them to an organization like Women of Worth or WEAVE so someone else can get use out of them. Your favorite navy pinstripe might be just what an abused woman needs for a job interview.

This is the dresser my parents bought me for my sixteenth birthday... That was how many years ago? And would you buy it today if you saw it in a store? If it's in decent shape, donate it to charity. It might be a treasure for a teenager whose worldly goods have been stowed in cardboard boxes. Many nonprofit organizations will even come to your home to pick up larger items, simplifying the process for you.

RANDOM ACTS OF KINDNESS

Giving back also means being generous and kind to the friends and family who surround you. So often we forget that respect, thoughtful words, listening, and laughter are direct pathways to love and happiness—to letting those closest to us know that we care about them.

Consider the long-term positive rewards that come from simple acts of kindness. Hug a friend who is upset. Call your uncle who's been ill and let him know you're thinking of him. Look in on your aging neighbor. Offer to babysit so your son and his wife can have a much-needed night out. Take care of your cousin's Rottweiler while she's having surgery. Give a good friend those pricey designer clothes that no longer fit you.

VOLUNTEERISM/COMMUNITY INVOLVEMENT

Time is a valuable commodity, and offering it generously is of great value to many nonprofits. Do a bit of research and find a local organization that speaks to your values, then volunteer an hour or two a week or a month—whatever feels right. Animal rescue shelters, national parks, food banks, Habitat for Humanity, libraries, museums, and retirement homes are some of the nonprofits that are always looking for volunteers. Not only will you be contributing to something that matters, but you'll probably meet some like-minded folks along the way. You'll also have a really good answer to the question most retired people dread: "What are you doing with all your free time?" It's far more satisfying to say you cook and serve meals at a homeless shelter than to stammer, "Oh, I knit...watch 'I Love Lucy' reruns on Netflix...walk the dog...babysit the grandkids." Talk about a conversation stopper! Remember—we're trying to make the most of the rest of our lives, not bide our time.

After twenty-five years of smoking, JoAnn decided it was time to stop. She enrolled in a class at a local hospital and was surprised to discover that the nurse who ran the program had never smoked. Because he wasn't intimately involved with the addictive pull of nicotine, he had limited credibility with the people who were taking his class.

JoAnn stayed on in spite of the instructor's limitations and successfully completed the program, even though several others dropped out. As a health educator, she recognized the soundness and efficacy of the program strategies, so to keep it going, she offered to teach future classes.

"I knew it would be easier for people to follow the advice of someone who has been there and beat the habit," she tells us. "Running the program is also a way for me to give back to my community by sharing what I have learned. There's enormous satisfaction in seeing class participants develop new habits and embrace a healthier lifestyle."

A little side note here: it is often in a woman's nature to give too much. Hear us when we say that there's never a legitimate reason to give until it hurts—or to give more time, money, or resources than you can afford. That's why we suggest deciding on a time limit before you volunteer your services.

If you are a retired teacher or an expert on a particular subject, one way to give back is to become a mentor. If you want some compelling reasons to add it to your repertoire, visit mentoring.com. According to the site, "Mentoring, at its core, guarantees young people that there is someone who cares about them, assures them they are not alone in dealing with day-to-day challenges, and makes them feel like they matter."

Do some research and find out what group in your community is the most vulnerable. Is it the homeless? The elderly and alone? Refugees? Determine who needs help the most, then direct your efforts accordingly.

For some people, the spirit of volunteerism takes on significant dimension. People can become motivated to support an issue when it unexpectedly becomes their own. Such was the case with Janice, who felt compelled to create a solution to a problem that affected both her community and her family.

Janice O'Brien

After spending thirteen years in a convent, Janice left to pursue a secular life. A year and a half later, she met the man who would one day become her husband. A widower whose wife had been killed by a lightning strike, Jim charmed Janice with his intelligence and quick wit.

In time they were married, and Janice adopted Jim's three little boys. It wasn't long before Peter was born, and the family of six settled into a happy life.

By the time Peter was fifteen, he was experimenting with marijuana and alcohol. He went into rehab for the first time at the age of eighteen—a pattern that would continue seven times over the next several years. He eventually married Jennifer, a woman who was addicted to pain pills. She had lost two children to Child Protective Services (CPS) because of her drug problem, but a third child remained with her. The couple had two more children and settled in Tacoma, Washington, but their respective addictions caused the family to fall into homelessness.

Jim and Janice kept in contact with their son and daughter-in-law as much as possible, but they were dealing with issues of their own. In 2001, Jim was diagnosed with prostate cancer—an issue that generated major changes in their lives, including retiring and moving to California's Sierra foothills. At the time, Janice was sixty-five years old.

Shortly after their arrival, they received word that CPS had removed Peter and Jennifer's three children from the home. To keep them out of foster care and to give them a safe environment, Janice and Jim agreed to take in the three little ones, who were five, three, and twenty months.

While the children settled into their new home with their grandparents, Peter and Jennifer continued their drug-and-alcohol lifestyle. Unable to hold down jobs, they were living in a van. Torn between sympathy for their plight and an unwillingness to come to their rescue, Jim and Janice suggested that the couple move to California and live in a tent on their property. It did not go well.

After tolerating vicious arguments, foul language, and altercations that would carry on well into the night, they told their son and his wife to leave. The homeless camps in the area became their temporary solution—albeit a very rough and dangerous one.

In search of a better answer for Peter and Jennifer and others like them, Janice joined a formidable group of advocates to found Hospitality House in Nevada City, California in October of 2005. An emergency homeless shelter committed to providing a place of safety and dignity to those in need of mental, emotional, and physical help, it was home to Peter and Jennifer as soon as the doors opened. A month after moving in, the couple spent Thanksgiving weekend with Janice, Jim, and the children, and hope seemed to bloom at last.

That Sunday, Jennifer wanted to stop by one of the homeless camps before returning to Hospitality House. When Janice and Jim took Peter to pick her up a few hours later, there was no sign of her.

Certain that she had managed to find a ride, they returned Peter to Hospitality House—but Jennifer was not there. Several days passed, and still there was no word from her. On December 3, 2005, she was officially declared a missing person.

Four years later, her remains were found in a shallow grave by a hiker. Rumors circulating in the homeless community said she got high at the camp, became belligerent, and was attacked and murdered by one of the residents. Because so much time had transpired between when she went missing and when she was found, the authorities had to take DNA samples from her children to confirm her identity.

Janice and Jim took Peter in at that point, and his life became a pattern of drunk/rehab/repeat. His drinking and poor personal habits eventually led to morbid obesity. In 2013, when Peter seemed willing to try again, Janice took him to a detox center. An hour after she dropped him off, he called to tell her he couldn't stay because there wasn't a bed big enough for him.

Janice returned to the center to get him, stopped at the hospital to pick up the meds that would allow him to detox at home, and brought him back to the house. He'd been there for four days when he called his daughters into his room and apologized for being a bad dad. After he made his amends, he went to sleep. When his younger daughter went in to check on him a few hours later, he was dead.

Although devastated by her son's passing, Janice saw the bigger picture: a critical need for a safe haven for the chronically homeless. While Hospitality House serves a significant purpose, it does not allow residents who aren't sober or who have animals, and it cannot accommodate people with physical disabilities.

"For whatever reason, there are many homeless and marginalized individuals who cannot—or will not—use the services of Hospitality House," she explains. "In spite of this, they still need help and connection to get well and become participating and accepted members of the community."

In late 2010, when a local homeless man froze to death under a bridge, Janice knew something had to be done. She resigned from the Hospitality House board and mobilized a group of volunteers to establish Sierra Roots—an organization dedicated to serving the homeless people whose needs are not being met elsewhere.

The ultimate goal of Sierra Roots is to build a village with access to private sleeping structures, showers, laundry facilities, and healthy food. Residents would actively contribute to the village's design, build-out, and operations— including organic gardens and orchards, an aquaponic greenhouse, beekeeping, and vermiculture.

"My son was the inspiration behind Sierra Roots," says Janice, "but it is now so much bigger than that. The individuals who use our services have become like family to me, and I am committed to ensuring that they have a safe, secure, and stable environment where they are linked to the appropriate supportive resources. By creating this sustainable, collaborative environment, we can help people in need work toward health, purpose, and self-reliance."

ACTION STEPS

I am willing to give more by taking the following action. (Check all that apply.)

I will find a charity I believe in and make at least one financial contribution that is within my means.

I will go through my closets and cupboards and donate items I no longer need or use.

I will look for one or more volunteer opportunities in my community.

I will find ways to perform frequent random acts of kindness for my family members, friends, and neighbors.

I will put together a will or trust or otherwise be responsible about who gets my prized possessions and family heirlooms.

I will make an effort to be kind, supportive, loving, generous, and appreciative as often as possible.

Chapter 9

Putting It All Together

"Life isn't meant to be lived perfectly...but merely to be lived. Boldly,
wildly, beautifully, uncertainly, imperfectly, magically lived."
— Mandy Hale, American author

So, ladies, here we are—approaching the end of this book. Before we put everything together into a plan that will help provide fulfillment for the rest of your life, let's talk about some of the things that might be stopping you.

Odds are, you've figure out by now that life is fraught with everyday annoyances and inevitable tragedies. In spite of our best efforts, pain and suffering prevail, problems both large and small rear their ugly heads, and "That really sucks" is a frequent mantra. You've learned from experience that the bad stuff will pass, but the challenge is getting through each predicament with a maximum of grace and a minimum of drama.

No matter what the circumstances are, you always have a choice. You might not have selected a particular situation, but you have the option of choosing what to do about it. You can decide to react as if the sky is falling, or you can maintain a sense of balance and respond like a reasonable adult. Many of us get this far in life only to feel as if we have given up control and it's futile to try to get what we want. But we can gain that elusive control—and a whopping heap of power—when we consciously choose how to respond to life's ups and downs.

Do you really have to get into yet another argument with your daughter about her lifestyle, boyfriends, deadbeat husband, or ill-behaved children? Does screaming obscenities at the driver who cut you off make you feel better, or does it only serve to raise your blood pressure? Will one more lecture about your husband being late, forgetting to pay the electric bill, or failing to fix the leaky faucet change anything? Is being right about anything or everything really that important? Instead of fighting the same old fight, take a few deep breaths and simply decide to let some of that bullshit go before it makes you sick—or sicker than you already are.

Olivia is fifty-eight, and although she has a wicked sense of humor, she isn't a particularly happy person. She suffers from migraines that she believes are caused by stress, and she admits that it's mostly self-induced. If you believe what she says, absolutely nothing in Olivia's life is right.

In the twenty years that we've known her, she's complained about her weight, haircuts, boyfriends, pets, mother, father, siblings, house, jobs, lack of jobs, finances, her wardrobe, hippies at the health food store, lack of good restaurants, the weather (it's too hot or too cold), joint pain, depression, and exhaustion. Most recently, her hot topics are her new husband and her mother-in-law. The former doesn't have enough money and is a momma's boy, and the latter is an "insensitive, meddling bitch."

To her credit, Olivia's monologues are humorous and make us wonder if she should consider pursuing a career as a stand-up comic. The sad truth, however, is that she's trapped in a vicious cycle of negativity that is affecting her health and well-being. Oh sure—she sees a therapist and is on antidepressants, but she still refuses to accept responsibility for her circumstances, blames everyone but herself, and responds to everything with a knee-jerk reaction. Her friends feel her pain and want to help, but Olivia is trapped. She is a victim, and complaining is easier than finding viable solutions. In fact, she's so trapped she can't even consider the options.

Granted, Olivia is an extreme example of someone who has relinquished control of her life, but on occasion, you may experience times when your inner Olivia takes hold. Trying to make plans for a fulfilling future puts you smack dab in front of old beliefs and behavior patterns that will thwart your progress or stop you dead in your tracks.

Let's say you really want to spend a month in Paris with your best friend—eating croissants, sipping *une noisette*, shopping, and practicing your very rusty high school French. You have the money, but your spouse isn't on board. Unencumbered by a sense of adventure, he wants you to stay home with him. In the past, his resistance to your proposed travel plans has caused your blood to boil, but you bit your tongue to avoid an argument, succumbed, and tossed your passport in the back of your sock drawer. But now, motivated to make the most of the rest of your life, you're determined to go. So how will you do it?

Get into a positive frame of mind, taking the time to be clear about what you want. Then, present your case in a way that is logical, unemotional, and respectful. The key to success is twofold: believing that you can get what you want and trying a new approach. If you continually apply old (and not particularly successful) patterns of behavior and expect a different (and better) outcome, you are doomed to fail.

Because most people are rooted in, and comfortable with, maintaining the status quo, it's common to subconsciously undermine your desires and inadvertently set yourself up to get precisely the reactions you are trying to avoid. Instead of picking your battles carefully, the tendency is to overreact to a situation and make it far worse than it needs to be.

Now—no more of that, okay? There are ways to overcome the attitudes and beliefs that can trip you up when your inner Olivia is in charge.

What follows is a list of character traits to help you develop the fortitude, stamina, and attitude to get you through the times when you need direction and strength, but your angel guides are on vacation and your intuition is lacking. Each word is a reminder of the options you have for taking the high road. How you use this chart is up to you, but here are some suggestions:

Read through the list from beginning to end and notice what trait speaks to you. Keep it in mind as you go through your day.

Or pick a trait at random and use it as a daily meditation.

Select a trait you know has the potential to change your life in a positive way and keep it in mind for days, weeks, or even months until it becomes an unconscious part of your being.

Pick three traits for the month, write them on sticky notes, and post them in highly visible spots.

Journal about the changes that occur by making these traits a prominent part of your daily thoughts and actions.

We've mentioned all of these traits in previous chapters, and there are many more positive attributes you could add. Whenever you're feeling hopeless or tempted to kick down a door, take a moment to peruse this chart to see if you might come up with behavior that's more creative and effective.

CHARACTER TRAITS	HOW TO ACHIEVE THEM
Accepting	Borrow from the 12-step recovery support groups: *God, grant me the serenity* *To accept the things I cannot change,* *Courage to change the things I can,* *and wisdom to know the difference.* Or simply embrace an attitude of live and let live.
Adaptable	Go with the flow and embrace change.
Appreciative	Say thank you out loud and often. Let your family and friends know when they do something that helps or pleases you. Express your gratitude for what they do.
Balanced	Make an effort to find the middle ground. Avoid black and white thinking. Nothing is all good or all bad. There is a range of emotion.
Brave	If you get a bad diagnosis, face a difficult challenge, or have to make a hard decision, don't whine about it. Ask questions, seek help, and do the best you can. Be strong.
Communicative	Speak your mind honestly, clearly, and as considerately as possible. Listen—really listen—to what others have to say.

Compassionate	Whenever you can, be caring, kind, loving, sweet, and understanding. Refrain from passing judgment, making negative comments, or instilling doubt. These are surefire ways to alienate others.
Coping	Learn to deal with whatever comes your way by being as positive as possible. It's okay to express your feelings and to have an emotional breakdown on occasion, but the ultimate goal is acceptance.
Courageous	No matter how much fear is coursing through your veins, stand up to whatever it is and fight back with all your might.
Curious	Stop thinking you know it all. Ask questions, learn new things, and seek out experts.
Enthusiastic	In any situation, project a zest for life. Have fun, laugh out loud, dare to be zany.
Flexible	Change requires the ability to adapt and adjust. Being rigid about anything causes stress and anxiety—to you and whomever else is involved.
Generous	If you have it to give, then give it: time, knowledge, food, things you love but don't use, money. You will never be sorry.
Goal-Driven	Keep yourself positive and vibrant by creating goals—both large and small—that will add interest and dimension to your life.
Good-Natured	Be as happy as you can be as often as possible. It draws people to you and makes them want to spend time with you.

Healthy	Make smart food choices, exercise regularly, limit alcohol consumption, don't smoke, and practice good hygiene.
Honest	If you can tell the truth without devastating another person, do it. If the truth hurts and there's no benefit involved, keep it to yourself.
Humorous	The best antidote to difficult aspects of life is laughter. If you can say something funny, it's usually appreciated (as long as it's appropriate).
Interested	Be curious. Ask open-ended questions to show that you want to know more about a person or subject.
Open and Friendly	Smile. Be receptive and available to answer questions and be of assistance. Let people know you're there for them.
Optimistic	See the upside of each situation. Imagine a positive outcome. Have faith. Believe.
Organized	Having your affairs in order will enable you to deal with things more easily and efficiently. Heck—even having your drawers, cupboards, and closets in order will simplify your life!
Patient	Breathe. The only time anything is a crisis is when you make it so. What do you have to do that is so damn important?
Positive	Generate an aura of love, acceptance, joy, fun—you know, good vibes. It will get you a lot more than negativity will.

Respectful	No matter who you were or what you did in the past, you're not so important or entitled that you can't give others their due. Listen. Avoid conflict. Walk away if you must.
Responsible	Own your behavior and make sure it's always appropriate. Whether managing relationships or money, behave like the responsible grownup you're supposed to be.
Self-Assured	Have confidence in your abilities and in your character. Be comfortable with who you are, and stop comparing yourself to others.

ABSOLUTION—HERE, NOW, AND FOREVER

We've all done things we regret: hurt people unnecessarily, lied when the truth would have been more effective, betrayed a friend, or worse. If these memories come back to haunt you or keep you up at night, we suggest you find a way to forgive yourself and move on. Making mistakes is part of life, and we've all had our share of them. If you need to apologize, go right ahead, but here's your get-out-of-jail-free card:

We hereby give you official permission to let go of any guilt and residual pain you've been carrying over something you did that was unconscious, rude, harmful, hurtful, illegal, stupid, or otherwise bad. You are formally absolved of this sin. No need to murmur a Hail Mary or Act of Contrition; no attendance at a Yom Kippur or Ramadan service required. It's simply time to make peace with the past and let whatever it is go—once and for all.

What really matters in the end is that your life has meaning and makes sense to you—that you've done the best you can with what you have. That's it. Everything else is icing on the cake. Now, it's time to do whatever brings you peace of mind and some enjoyment.

Throughout this book, we've encouraged you to look at the various aspects of your life to determine what has worked, what has brought you joy, what still needs to be done, and where you would like to go from here. In retrospect, a good life is really about having a sense of balance and completion, so let go of the things that hold you back and prevent you from really living. You can do this. You're almost there!

CREATING YOUR PLAN

We're hoping you've completed the action steps at the end of each chapter, because they're there to inspire you. Now we'd like you to go back and pick one to three steps from each chapter. Here's an example of what your individual chart might look like:

SAMPLE PLAN	
Physical Wellness	I will get to my ideal weight. I will go to the gym at least three times a week to dance, lift weights, and stretch.
Emotional Health	I will stop using alcohol to numb my boredom and my feelings. I will seek other options for my evenings, such as meditation, walking, or reading.
Finances	I will set aside a time to go over the household accounts with my spouse. (Bottle of wine to help get through it: optional) I will stop being so quick to offer money to friends, especially those who rely on my generosity instead of making it on their own.
Relationships	I will make a date with a friend at least once a week for coffee, tea, or lunch. I will host at least one dinner each month.

Behaviors	I will make a note of the things I complain about.
	I will look for realistic solutions to my problems.
	I will meditate daily for a minimum of fifteen minutes.
Appearance	I will try on all of my clothes and get rid of any that are unflattering or don't fit.
Learning Something New	I will spend ten minutes each day brushing up on my Spanish by using the language app I downloaded onto my phone six month ago and haven't looked at since.
	I will look for a class to take at the community college.
Giving Back	I will continue to help my son launch his business.
	I will research long-term giving options.
Fun	I will do something enjoyable every day.
	I will plan a trip to Costa Rica with my husband.
	I will plan a trip to Cuba with my girlfriends.
Putting It All Together	I will review and update this list on the last day of each month.

Even if you're an overachieving, highly competitive perfectionist, select tasks that are easy to accomplish in one month or less. Once you get into the habit of planning and following through with the various activities, you can add steps that are more complicated.

CONCLUSION

What you do with the rest of your life is really your call. At this point, you've paid enough dues and learned enough lessons to enjoy the ride. While we stress balance, there's absolutely nothing wrong with a little outrage or excess.

Gone are the days—or at least they should be—when you beat yourself up over anything. Good for you if you finally speak your mind or ask for what you want. Props if you get rid of those hideous family heirlooms or paint the living room wall red.

So what if you serve Thanksgiving dinner on paper plates because you hate cleaning up? What does it matter if you opt to stay in bed until noon reading your favorite author? Who cares if you go out to dinner in yoga pants? (Oh, wait. Elle does. We need to get back to you on that one.)

Regardless of your age, you're only as old as you feel. If Lady Gaga is your thing, horrify your kids and go to her next concert. Take swing dancing or Zydeco lessons. If you always wanted to be a rock star, become a regular on karaoke night at the local bar. If there's something you want to do and you have the means, we encourage you to go do it. Whatever you do, don't stop now. There is still time to make the most of the rest of your life.

Cheryl is a perfect example of someone who makes up her mind and follows through. Nothing is going to get in her way, and the result is that she accomplishes precisely what she sets out to do.

Cheryl Acheson

Like many mothers whose children leave the nest, Cheryl found herself with an abundance of time and energy that needed an outlet. She wanted to make a contribution to the world...to be part of something...but she was unclear how to proceed. The thought of resuming her former role in corporate marketing held no appeal or excitement. Also, after spending years raising a family, she wasn't sure she had the skills to go back to the same job. After much research and soul-searching, she took a leap of faith and decided to try to turn her love of yoga into a new career at the age of fifty-one.

Cheryl meekly approached her yoga instructor and told him that she might want to teach. Much to her surprise, he was thrilled and supportive. She began by working as his in-class apprentice to see if the role of teacher was as fulfilling as she'd hoped. And it was. For the next three years, she took on more teaching responsibilities under his supervision—leading classes and gathering the critical feedback that would help take her skills to the next level.

"After a year of apprenticing and with the confidence of the naive, I approached the studio's owner about an official teaching position. My newly expanding bubble deflated a bit when I was told that I would first have to complete a 200-hour certified yoga-instructor training course.

"Fortunately, I found a program nearby—one of the advantages of living in the yoga vortex of California. The course work included history and philosophy lectures, hands-on anatomy sessions, and time on the mat learning about different types of yoga. I attended night lectures, devoted weekends to all-day studio classes, and was closely monitored by staff teachers. After five months and a cost of $1,600, I was certified through the Yoga Alliance, an international yoga-training organization.

"Since then, I have completed an additional 120 hours of teacher training in various yoga disciplines, including classes designed exclusively for children. Although this additional instruction is not a certification requirement, it helps make my teaching more comprehensive and dynamic.

"I now teach a total of ten classes each week at four different yoga studios—including the one where I apprenticed—and also give private lessons. My oldest student is eighty and the youngest is four, and every person I teach brings me complete joy and satisfaction. Perhaps most important of all, I have managed to enrich my life while helping others reap the physiological, psychological, and biochemical rewards of yoga."

CHERYL'S ADVICE FOR APPROACHING A CAREER CHANGE

Make a commitment to reinvent yourself and go public with it. Tell your family and friends and ask for their support. Doing so makes you accountable to them, and that fact alone may spur you on to pursue your dream. After all, if your holier-than-thou neighbor asks how your new career is going, you don't want to have to tell her you're spending all your time eating bonbons and watching the Lifetime channel.

Have a game plan with a final goal and stick with it, taking the necessary steps to get where you want to go. Kick your imagination into gear and visualize yourself in your new role.

Don't be afraid to revise your plan. I thought I would teach Anusara yoga exclusively, but I soon realized that I enjoy learning and sharing different styles. You can be flexible without veering off the main track.

Get a credential or certification, if required, to show that you're serious about your new profession.

Be creative. I market my services through my website, send out monthly news-letters, and also use social networking. Things like Facebook and blogging challenge me, but I enjoy learning about these aspects of marketing.

Addendum

Creating Your Plan

Now it's time to design your own personal action plan. To simplify the process, go back to the sample plan and write yours for the upcoming month. Be as specific and realistic as you can, then hold yourself accountable.

At the end of the month, evaluate your course and adjust it, if necessary. Answer the following questions:

> Did you stick to the plan? If yes, hooray for you! Now create your plan for the next month.

> If you didn't stick to the plan, what stopped you?

> What did you do to overcome the obstacles you encountered?

At the end of a year, you just might be amazed at what you've accomplished.

Some advice to follow: when you're developing your plan, do what optimists do. Focus on your passion. Make a decision to step into your life and embrace what's going on. Once you decide on a direction, follow it. Be flexible, because life is what happens when you're making other plans.

In the words of the fabulous Sophia Loren, a sage in her own right, "There is a fountain of youth: it is your mind, your talents, the creativity you bring to your life and the lives of the people you love. When you learn to tap this source, you will truly have defeated age."

Endnotes

1. "Physical Wellness," Stanford Health Care, healthysteps4u.org

2. "Alcohol: If you drink, keep it moderate," Mayo Clinic, mayoclinic.org

3. mountaineers.org

4. mazamas.org

5. sierraclub.org

6. "100 million Americans live with chronic pain, but treatment research is insufficient," Indiana University study, 2015, Science Daily, sciencedaily.com

7. "Depression In Older Adults: More Facts," Mental Health America, mentalhealthamerica.net

8. "Mental Health By The Numbers," National Alliance on Mental Illness, nami.org

9. Jesse Singal, "Going From Extremely Lazy to Pretty Lazy Could Be Lifesaving," New York Magazine, thecut.com

10. Emma M. Seppälä, PhD, "20 Scientific Reasons to Start Meditating Today," Psychology Today, psychologytoday.com

11. "Breathing Techniques for Stress Relief," WebMD, webmd.com

12. Barbara A. Friedberg, "Are We in a Baby Boomer Retirement Crisis?" Investopedia, investopedia.com

13. Michelle Fabio, Esq., "Top Three Benefits of a Living Trust," Legal Zoom, legalzoom.com

14. Jessica Ainlay and Dani Heinrich, *Break Free: The Ultimate Guide to Housesitting*, Amazon Digital Services, 2013

15. Liz Mineo, "Good genes are nice, but joy is better," The Harvard Gazette, news.harvard.edu

16   goaheadtours.com

17   "It's never too late to be a Volunteer," Peace Corps, peacecorps.gov

18   "Gone with the Wind," 1939, written by Sidney Howard, based on the novel by Margaret Mitchell

19   enneagraminstitute.com

20   myersbriggs.org

21   "Home Organization," Angie's List, angieslist.com

22   "Compression Wear and Shapewear Market Overview," Allied Market Research, alliedmarketresearch.com

23   Sam Saboura, Real Style: Style Secrets for Real Women with Real Bodies (Clarkson Potter, 2005)

24   "The Most Affordable Online Colleges in 2018," AC Online, affordblecollegesonline.org

25   Lauren Silverman, "Learning a New Skill Works Best to Keep Your Brain Sharp," NPR, npr.org

26   Alison Pearce Stevens, "Learning rewires the brain," Science News for Students, sciencenewsforstudents.org

27   Heidi Godman, "Regular Exercise Changes the Brain to Improve Memory, Thinking Skills," Harvard Health Publications, Harvard Medical School, 2016

L. (Elle) Gianforte is an award-winning writer with experience in both the advertising and publishing arenas. Her copywriting career extends from New York to London to California, including work for a diversity of business-to-consumer clients. She is also a collaborative author, ghostwriter, and developmental editor, and several of her books have been written under the name L.G. Mansfield. The genres she has worked in include lifestyle, fashion, interior design, self-help, adoption, memoir, and food. She earned her BA degree in English from Kean University in New Jersey and attended the School of Visual Arts in New York.

Jan Fishler began her career writing and producing informational and motivational videos. In addition to developing more than 100 corporate scripts, she produced *"The Path to Publication"* DVD series. Filmed at the Community of Writers Conference at Squaw Valley, the series contains advice from authors that include Amy Tan, Anne Lamott, Janet Fitch, and Mark Childress. In 2010, she self-published an adoption memoir, *Searching for Jane, Finding Myself.* She has written for *VietNow National Magazine* and *The Union* newspaper in Grass Valley, California. She has a BS in English literature from Ohio University and an MA in educational technology from California State University, San Francisco.

We invite you to be part of our community of smart women, and we're always delighted to hear from our followers. Please subscribe to our website and blog at dontstopnow.us and visit our Facebook page: @DontStopNow.thebook.

Made in the USA
Columbia, SC
19 November 2021

49086115R00078